HESIOD

THE THEOGONY

WORKS AND DAYS

TRANSLATED BY HUGH G. EVELYN-WHITE

Copyright © 2022 Aziloth Books

All Rights Reserved. No part of this publication may be reproduced, stored in a retrieval system or transmitted in any form or by any means, electronic, mechanical, photocopying, recording, scanning or otherwise, except under the terms of the Copyright Licensing Agency Ltd, 90 Tottenham Court Road, London, W1P 0LP, UK, without the permission in writing of the Publisher. Requests to the Publisher should be via email to: info@azilothbooks.com.

Every effort has been made to contact all copyright holders. The publisher will be glad to make good in future editions any errors or omissions brought to their attention.

This publication is designed to provide authoritative and accurate information in regard to the subject matter covered. It is sold on the understanding that the Publisher is not engaged in rendering professional services. If professional advice or other expert assistance is required, the services of a competent professional should be sought.

British Library Cataloguing in Publication Data

A catalogue record for this book is available from the British Library

ISBN-13: 978-1-913751-91-3

Cover Illustration:
Les Voix (Hesiod and the Muse)
Gustave Moreau (1880).

CONTENTS

INTRODUCTION	5
Endnotes	19
THE THEOGENY	21
Endnotes	49
WORKS AND DAYS	53
Endnotes	77

Hesiod & the Muse
Gustav Moreau (1858)

INTRODUCTION

General

The early Greek epic – that is, poetry as a natural and popular, and not (as it became later) an artificial and academic literary form – passed through the usual three phases, of development, of maturity, and of decline.

No fragments which can be identified as belonging to the first period survive to give us even a general idea of the history of the earliest epic, and we are therefore thrown back upon the evidence of analogy from other forms of literature and of inference from the two great epics which have come down to us. So reconstructed, the earliest period appears to us as a time of slow development in which the characteristic epic metre, diction, and structure grew up slowly from crude elements and were improved until the verge of maturity was reached.

The second period, which produced the *Iliad* and the *Odyssey*, needs no description here: but it is very important to observe the effect of these poems on the course of post-Homeric epic. As the supreme perfection and universality of the *Iliad* and the *Odyssey* cast into oblivion whatever pre-Homeric poets had essayed, so these same qualities exercised a paralysing influence over the successors of Homer. If they continued to sing like their great predecessor of romantic themes, they were drawn as by a kind of magnetic attraction into the Homeric style and manner of treatment, and became mere echoes of the Homeric voice: in a word, Homer had so completely exhausted the epic *genre*, that after him further efforts were doomed to be merely conventional. Only the rare and exceptional genius of Vergil and Milton could use the Homeric medium without loss of individuality: and this quality none of the later epic poets seem to have possessed. Freedom from the domination of the great tradition could only be found by seeking new subjects, and such freedom was really only illusionary, since romantic subjects alone are suitable for epic treatment.

In its third period, therefore, epic poetry shows two divergent tendencies. In Ionia and the islands the epic poets followed the Homeric tradition, singing of romantic subjects in the now stereotyped heroic style, and showing originality only in their choice of legends hitherto neglected or summarily and imperfectly treated. In continental Greece[1], on the other hand, but especially in Boeotia, a new form of epic sprang up, which for the romance and PATHOS of the Ionian School substituted the practical and matter-of-fact. It dealt in moral and practical maxims, in information on technical subjects which are of service in daily life – agriculture, astronomy, augury, and the calendar – in matters of religion and in tracing the genealogies of men. Its attitude is summed up in the words of the Muses to the writer of the Theogony: 'We can tell many a feigned tale to look like truth, but we can, when we will, utter the truth' (*Theogony* 26-27). Such a poetry could not be permanently successful, because the subjects of which it treats – if susceptible of poetic treatment at all – were certainly not suited for epic treatment, where unity of action which will sustain interest, and to which each part should contribute, is absolutely necessary. While, therefore, an epic like the Odyssey is an organism and dramatic in structure, a work such as the Theogony is a merely artificial collocation of facts, and, at best, a pageant. It is not surprising, therefore, to find that from the first the Boeotian school is forced to season its matter with romantic episodes, and that later it tends more and more to revert (as in the *Shield of Heracles*) to the Homeric tradition.

The Boeotian School

How did the continental school of epic poetry arise? There is little definite material for an answer to this question, but the probability is that there were at least three contributory causes. First, it is likely that before the rise of the Ionian epos there existed in Boeotia a purely popular and indigenous poetry of a crude form: it comprised, we may suppose, versified proverbs and precepts relating to life in general, agricultural maxims, weather-lore, and the like. In this sense the Boeotian poetry may be taken to have its germ in maxims similar to our English

> *"Till May be out, ne'er cast a clout,"*
>
> or
>
> *"A rainbow in the morning*
> *Is the Shepherd's warning."*

Secondly and thirdly we may ascribe the rise of the new epic to the nature of the Boeotian people and, as already remarked, to a spirit of revolt against the old epic. The Boeotians, people of the class of which Hesiod represents himself to be the type, were essentially unromantic; their daily needs marked the general limit of their ideals, and, as a class, they cared little for works of fancy, for pathos, or for fine thought as such. To a people of this nature the Homeric epos would be inacceptable, and the post-Homeric epic, with its conventional atmosphere, its trite and hackneyed diction, and its insincere sentiment, would be anathema. We can imagine, therefore, that among such folk a settler, of Aeolic origin like Hesiod, who clearly was well acquainted with the Ionian epos, would naturally see that the only outlet for his gifts lay in applying epic poetry to new themes acceptable to his hearers.

Though the poems of the Boeotian school [2] were unanimously assigned to Hesiod down to the age of Alexandrian criticism, they were clearly neither the work of one man nor even of one period: some, doubtless, were fraudulently fathered on him in order to gain currency; but it is probable that most came to be regarded as his partly because of their general character, and partly because the names of their real authors were lost. One fact in this attribution is remarkable – the veneration paid to Hesiod.

Life of Hesiod

Our information respecting Hesiod is derived in the main from notices and allusions in the works attributed to him, and to these must be added traditions concerning his death and burial gathered from later writers.

Hesiod's father (whose name, by a perversion of *Works and Days*, 299 Πέρση δῖου γένος to Πέρση, Δίου γένος, was thought to have been Dius) was a native of Cyme in Aeolis, where he was a seafaring trader and, perhaps, also a farmer. He was forced by poverty to leave his native place, and returned to continental Greece, where he settled at Ascra near Thespiae in Boeotia (*Works and Days*, 636 ff.). Either in Cyme or Ascra, two sons, Hesiod and Perses, were born to the settler, and these, after his death, divided the farm between them. Perses, however, who is represented as an idler and spendthrift, obtained and kept the larger share by bribing the corrupt 'lords' who ruled from Thespiae (*Works and Days*, 37-39). While his brother wasted his patrimony and ultimately came to want (*Works and Days*, 34 ff.), Hesiod lived a farmer's life until, according to the very early tradition preserved by the author of the *Theogony* (22-23), the Muses met him as he was tending sheep on Mt. Helicon and "taught him a glorious song" – doubtless the *Works and Days*. The only other personal reference is to his victory in a poetical contest at the funeral games of Amphidamas at Chalcis in Euboea, where he won the prize, a tripod, which he dedicated to the Muses of Helicon (*Works and Days*, 651-9).

Before we go on to the story of Hesiod's death, it will be well to inquire how far the "autobiographical" notices can be treated as historical, especially as many critics treat some, or all of them, as spurious. In the first place attempts have been made to show that "Hesiod" is a significant name and therefore fictitious: it is only necessary to mention Goettling's derivation from ἵημι to ὁδός (which would make 'Hesiod' mean the 'guide' in virtues and technical arts), and to refer to the pitiful attempts in the *Etymologicum Magnu* (s.v. Ἡσίοδος), to show how prejudiced and lacking even in plausibility such efforts are. It seems certain that 'Hesiod' stands as a proper name in the fullest sense. Secondly, Hesiod claims that his father – if not he himself – came from Aeolis and settled in Boeotia. There is fairly definite evidence to warrant our acceptance of this: the dialect of the *Works and Days* is shown by Rzach[3] to contain distinct Aeolisms apart from those which formed part of the general stock of epic poetry. And that this Aeolic speaking poet was a Boeotian of Ascra seems even more certain, since the tradition is never once disputed, insignificant though the place was, even before its destruction by the Thespians.

Again, Hesiod's story of his relations with his brother Perses have been treated with scepticism (see Murray, *Anc. Gk. Literature*, pp. 53-54): Perses, it is urged, is clearly a mere dummy, set up to be the target for the poet's exhortations. On such a matter precise evidence is naturally not forthcoming; but all probability is against the sceptical view. For: 1) if the quarrel between the brothers were a fiction, we should expect it to be detailed at length and not noticed allusively and rather obscurely – as we find it; 2) as MM. Croiset remark, if the poet needed a lay-figure the ordinary practice was to introduce some mythological person – as, in fact, is done in the *Precepts of Chiron*. In a word, there is no more solid ground for treating Perses and his quarrel with Hesiod as fictitious than there would be for treating Cyrnus, the friend of Theognis, as mythical.

Thirdly, there is the passage in the *Theogony* relating to Hesiod and the Muses. It is surely an error to suppose that lines 22-35 all refer to Hesiod: rather, the author of the *Theogony* tells the story of his own inspiration by the same Muses who once taught Hesiod glorious song. The lines 22-3 are therefore a very early piece of tradition about Hesiod, and though the appearance of Muses must be treated as a graceful fiction, we find that a writer, later than the *Works and Days* by perhaps no more than three-quarters of a century, believed in the actuality of Hesiod and in his life as a farmer or shepherd.

Lastly, there is the famous story of the contest in song at Chalcis. In later times the modest version in the *Works and Days* was elaborated, first by making Homer the opponent whom Hesiod conquered, while a later period exercised its ingenuity in working up the story of the contest into the elaborate form in which it still survives. Finally the contest, in which the two poets contended with hymns to Apollo[4], was transferred to Delos. These developments certainly need no consideration: are we to say the same of the passage in the *Works and Days*? Critics from Plutarch downwards have almost unanimously rejected the lines 654-662, on the ground that Hesiod's Amphidamas is the hero of the Lelantine Wars between Chalcis and Eretria, whose death may be placed circa 705 B.C. – a date which is obviously too low for the genuine Hesiod. Nevertheless, there is much to be said in defence of the passage. Hesiod's claim in the *Works and Days* is modest, since he neither pretends to have met Homer, nor to have sung in any but an impromptu, local festival, so that the supposed interpolation lacks a sufficient motive. And there is nothing in the context to show that Hesiod's Amphidamas is to be identified with that Amphidamas whom Plutarch alone connects with the Lelantine War: the name may have been borne by an earlier Chalcidian, an ancestor, perhaps, of the person to whom Plutarch refers.

The story of the end of Hesiod may be told in outline. After the contest at Chalcis, Hesiod went to Delphi and there was warned that the 'issue of death should overtake him in the fair grove of Nemean Zeus.' Avoiding therefore Nemea on the Isthmus of Corinth, to which he supposed the oracle to refer, Hesiod retired to Oenoe in Locris where he was entertained by Amphiphanes and Ganyetor, sons of a certain Phegeus. This place, however, was also sacred to Nemean Zeus, and the poet, suspected by his hosts of having seduced their sister [5], was murdered there. His body, cast into the sea, was brought to shore by dolphins and buried at Oenoe (or, according to Plutarch, at Ascra): at a later time his bones were removed to Orchomenus. The whole story is full of miraculous elements, and the various authorities disagree on numerous points of detail. The tradition seems, however, to be constant in declaring that Hesiod was murdered and buried at Oenoe, and in this respect it is at least as old as the time of Thucydides. In conclusion it may be worth while to add the graceful epigram of Alcaeus of Messene (*Palatine Anthology*, vii 55).

When in the shady Locrian grove Hesiod lay dead, the Nymphs washed his body with water from their own springs, and heaped high his grave; and thereon the goat-herds sprinkled offerings of milk mingled with yellow-honey: such was the utterance of the nine Muses that he breathed forth, that old man who had tasted of their pure springs.

The Hesiodic Poems

The Hesiodic poems fall into two groups according as they are didactic (technical or gnomic) or genealogical: the first group centres round the *Works and Days*, the second round the *Theogony*.

I. "The Works and Days"

The poem consists of four main sections. (*a*) After the prelude, which Pausanias failed to find in the ancient copy engraved on lead seen by him on Mt. Helicon, comes a general exhortation to industry. It begins with the allegory of the two Strifes, who stand for wholesome Emulation and Quarrelsomeness respectively. Then by means of the Myth of Pandora the poet shows how evil and the need for work first arose, and goes on to describe the Five Ages of the World, tracing the gradual increase in evil, and emphasizing the present miserable condition of the world, a condition in which struggle is inevitable. Next, after the Fable of the Hawk and Nightingale, which serves as a condemnation of violence and injustice, the poet passes on to contrast the blessing which Righteousness brings to a nation, and the punishment which Heaven sends down upon the violent, and the section concludes with a series of precepts on industry and prudent conduct generally. (*b*) The second section shows how a man may escape want and misery by industry and care both in agriculture and in trading by sea. Neither subject, it should be carefully noted, is treated in any way comprehensively. (*c*) The third part is occupied with miscellaneous precepts relating mostly to actions of domestic and everyday life and conduct which have little or no connection with one another. (*d*) The final section is taken up with a series of notices on the days of the month which are favourable or unfavourable for agricultural and other operations.

It is from the second and fourth sections that the poem takes its name. At first sight such a work seems to be a miscellany of myths, technical advice, moral precepts, and folklore maxims without any unifying principle; and critics have readily taken the view that the whole is a cento of fragments or short poems worked up by a redactor. Very probably Hesiod used much material of a far older date, just as Shakespeare used the *Gesta Romanorum*, old chronicles, and old plays; but close inspection will show that the *Works and Days* has a real unity and that the picturesque title is somewhat misleading. The poem has properly no technical object at all, but is moral: its real aim is to show men how best to live in a difficult world. So viewed the four seemingly independent sections will be found to be linked together in a real bond of unity. Such a connection between the first and second sections is easily seen, but the links between these and the third and fourth are no less real: to make life go tolerably smoothly it is most important to be just and to know how to win a livelihood; but happiness also largely depends on prudence and care both in social and home life as well, and not least on avoidance of actions which offend supernatural powers and bring ill-luck. And finally, if your industry is to be fruitful, you must know what days are suitable for various kinds of work. This moral aim – as opposed to the currently accepted technical aim of the poem – explains the otherwise puzzling incompleteness of the instructions on farming and seafaring.

Of the Hesiodic poems similar in character to the *Works and Days*, only the scantiest fragments survive. One at least of these, the *Divination by Birds*, was, as we know from Proclus, attached to the end of the *Works* until it was rejected by Apollonius Rhodius: doubtless it continued the same theme of how to live, showing how man can avoid disasters by attending to the omens to be drawn from birds. It is possible that the *Astronomy* or *Astrology* (as Plutarch calls it) was in turn appended to the *Divination*. It certainly gave some account of the principal constellations, their dates of rising and setting, and the legends connected with them, and probably showed how these influenced human affairs or might be used as guides. The *Precepts of Chiron* was a didactic poem made up of moral and practical precepts, resembling the gnomic sections of the *Works and Days*, addressed by the Centaur Chiron to his pupil Achilles. Even less is known of the poem called the *Great Works*: the title implies that it was similar in subject to the second section of the *Works and Days*, but longer. Possible references in Roman writers[6] indicate that among the subjects dealt with were the cultivation of the vine and olive and various herbs. The inclusion of the judgment of Rhadamanthys (frag. 1): "If a man sow evil, he shall reap evil," indicates a gnomic element, and the note by Proclus[7] on *Works and Days* 126 makes it likely that metals also were dealt with. It is therefore possible that another lost poem, the *Idaean Dactyls*, which dealt with the discovery of metals and their working, was appended to, or even was a part of the *Great Works*, just as the *Divination by Birds* was appended to the *Works and Days*.

II. The Genealogical Poems

The only complete poem of the genealogical group is the *Theogony*, which traces from the beginning of things the descent and vicissitudes of the families of the gods. Like the *Works and Days* this poem has no dramatic plot; but its unifying principle is clear and simple. The gods are classified chronologically: as soon as one generation is catalogued, the poet goes on to detail the offspring of each member of that generation. Exceptions are only made in special cases, as the Sons of Iapetus (ll. 507-616) whose place is accounted for by their treatment by Zeus. The chief landmarks in the poem are as follows: after the first 103 lines, which contain at least three distinct preludes, three primeval beings are introduced, Chaos, Earth, and Eros – here an indefinite reproductive influence. Of these three, Earth produces Heaven to whom she bears the Titans, the Cyclopes and the hundred-handed giants. The Titans, oppressed by their father, revolt at the instigation of Earth, under the leadership of Cronos, and as a result Heaven and Earth are separated, and Cronos reigns over the universe. Cronos, knowing that he is destined to be overcome by one of his children, swallows each one of them as they are born, until Zeus, saved by Rhea, grows up and overcomes Cronos in some struggle which is not described. Cronos is forced to vomit up the children he had swallowed, and these with Zeus divide the universe between them, like a human estate. Two events mark the early reign of Zeus, the war with the Titans and the overthrow of Typhoeus, and as Zeus is still reigning the poet can only go on to give a list of gods born to Zeus by various goddesses. After this he formally bids farewell to the cosmic and Olympian deities and enumerates the sons born of goddess to mortals. The poem closes with an invocation of the Muses to sing of the "tribe of women".

This conclusion served to link the *Theogony* to what must have been a distinct poem, the *Catalogues of Women*. This work was divided into four (Suidas says five) books, the last one (or two) of which was known as the *Eoiae* and may have been again a distinct poem: the curious title will be explained presently. The *Catalogues* proper were a series of genealogies which traced the Hellenic race (or its more important peoples and families) from a common ancestor. The reason why women are so prominent is obvious: since most families and tribes claimed to be descended from a god, the only safe clue to their origin was through a mortal woman beloved by that god; and it has also been pointed out that *mutterrecht* still left its traces in northern Greece in historical times.

The following analysis (after Marckscheffel) [8] will show the principle of its composition. From Prometheus and Pronoia sprang Deucalion and Pyrrha, the only survivors of the deluge, who had a son Hellen (frag. 1), the reputed ancestor of the whole Hellenic race. From the daughters of Deucalion sprang Magnes and Macedon, ancestors of the Magnesians and Macedonians, who are thus represented as cousins to the true Hellenic stock. Hellen had three sons, Dorus, Xuthus, and Aeolus, parents of the Dorian, Ionic and Aeolian races, and the offspring of these was then detailed. In one instance a considerable and characteristic section can be traced from extant fragments and notices: Salmoneus, son of Aeolus, had a daughter Tyro who bore to Poseidon two sons, Pelias and Neleus; the latter of these, king of Pylos, refused Heracles purification for the murder of Iphitus, whereupon Heracles attacked and sacked Pylos, killing amongst the other sons of Neleus Periclymenus, who had the power of changing himself into all manner of shapes. From this slaughter Neleus alone escaped (frags. 13, and 10-12). This summary shows the general principle of arrangement of the *Catalogues*: each line seems to have been dealt with in turn, and the monotony was relieved as far as possible by a brief relation of famous adventures connected with any of the personages – as in the case of Atalanta and Hippomenes (frag. 14). Similarly the story of the Argonauts appears from the fragments (37-42) to have been told in some detail.

This tendency to introduce romantic episodes led to an important development. Several poems are ascribed to Hesiod, such as the *Epithalamium of Peleus and Thetis*, the *Descent of Theseus into Hades*, or the *Circuit of the Earth* (which must have been connected with the story of Phineus and the Harpies, and so with the Argonaut-legend), which yet seem to have belonged to the *Catalogues*. It is highly probable that these poems were interpolations into the *Catalogues* expanded by later poets from more summary notices in the genuine Hesiodic work and subsequently detached from their contexts and treated as independent. This is definitely known to be true of the *Shield of Heracles*, the first 53 lines of which belong to the fourth book of the *Catalogues*, and almost certainly applies to other episodes, such as the *Suitors of Helen*[9], the *Daughters of Leucippus*, and the *Marriage of Ceyx*, which last Plutarch mentions as "interpolated in the works of Hesiod."

To the *Catalogues*, as we have said, was appended another work, the *Eoiae*. The title seems to have arisen in the following way[10]: the *Catalogues* probably ended (ep. *Theogony* 963 ff.) with some such passage as this: "But now, ye Muses, sing of the tribes of women with whom the Sons of Heaven were joined in love, women pre-eminent above their fellows in beauty, such as was Niobe (?)." Each succeeding heroine was then introduced by the formula "Or such as was..." (cp. frags. 88, 92, etc.). A large fragment of the *Eoiae* is extant at the beginning of the *Shield of Heracles*, which may be mentioned here. The "supplement" (ll. 57-480) is nominally Heracles and Cycnus, but the greater part is taken up with an inferior description of the shield of Heracles, in imitation of the Homeric shield of Achilles (*Iliad* xviii. 478 ff.). Nothing shows more clearly the collapse of the principles of the Hesiodic school than this ultimate servile dependence upon Homeric models.

At the close of the *Shield* Heracles goes on to Trachis to the house of Ceyx, and this warning suggests that the *Marriage of Ceyx* may have come immediately after the 'Or such as was' of Alcmena in the *Eoiae*: possibly Halcyone, the wife of Ceyx, was one of the heroines sung in the poem, and the original section was "developed" into the *Marriage*, although what form the poem took is unknown.

Next to the *Eoiae* and the poems which seemed to have been developed from it, it is natural to place the *Great Eoiae*. This, again, as we know from fragments, was a list of heroines who bare children to the gods: from the title we must suppose it to have been much longer than the simple *Eoiae*, but its extent is unknown. Lehmann, remarking that the heroines are all Boeotian and Thessalian (while the heroines of the *Catalogues* belong to all parts of the Greek world), believes the author to have been either a Boeotian or Thessalian.

Two other poems are ascribed to Hesiod. Of these the *Aegimius* (also ascribed by Athenaeus to Cercops of Miletus), is thought by Valckenaer to deal with the war of Aegimus against the Lapithae and the aid furnished to him by Heracles, and with the history of Aegimius and his sons. Otto Muller suggests that the introduction of Thetis and of Phrixus (frags. 1-2) is to be connected with notices of the allies of the Lapithae from Phthiotis and Iolchus, and that the story of Io was incidental to a narrative of Heracles' expedition against Euboea. The remaining poem, the *Melampodia*, was a work in three books, whose plan it is impossible to recover. Its subject, however, seems to have been the histories of famous seers like Mopsus, Calchas, and Teiresias, and it probably took its name from Melampus, the most famous of them all.

Date of the Hesiodic Poems

There is no doubt that the *Works and Days* is the oldest, as it is the most original, of the Hesiodic poems. It seems to be distinctly earlier than the *Theogony*, which refers to it, apparently, as a poem already renowned. Two considerations help us to fix a relative date for the *Works*.

(1) In diction, dialect and style it is obviously dependent upon Homer, and is therefore considerably later than the *Iliad* and *Odyssey*: moreover, as we have seen, it is in revolt against the romantic school, already grown decadent, and while the digamma is still living, it is obviously growing weak, and is by no means uniformly effective.

(2) On the other hand while tradition steadily puts the Cyclic poets at various dates from 776 B.C. downwards, it is equally consistent in regarding Homer and Hesiod as "prehistoric". Herodotus indeed puts both poets 400 years before his own time; that is, at about 830-820 B.C., and the evidence stated above points to the middle of the ninth century as the probable date for the Works and Days. The *Theogony* might be tentatively placed a century later; and the *Catalogues* and *Eoiae* are again later, but not greatly later, than the *Theogony*: the *Shield of Heracles* may be ascribed to the later half of the seventh century, but there is not evidence enough to show whether the other "developed" poems are to be regarded as of a date so low as this.

Literary Value of Hesiod

Quintillian's[11] judgment on Hesiod that "he rarely rises to great heights... and to him is given the palm in the middle-class of speech" is just, but is liable to give a wrong impression. Hesiod has nothing that remotely approaches such scenes as that between Priam and Achilles, or the pathos of Andromache's preparations for Hector's return, even as he was falling before the walls of Troy; but in matters that come within the range of ordinary experience, he rarely fails to rise to the appropriate level. Take, for instance, the description of the Iron Age (*Works and Days*, 182 ff.) with its catalogue of wrongdoings and violence ever increasing until Aidôs and Nemesis are forced to leave mankind who thenceforward shall have 'no remedy against evil'. Such occasions, however, rarely occur and are perhaps not characteristic of Hesiod's genius: if we would see Hesiod at his best, in his most natural vein, we must turn to such a passage as that which he himself – according to the compiler of the *Contest of Hesiod and Homer* – selected as best in all his work, 'When the Pleiades, Atlas' daughters, begin to rise...' (*Works and Days*, 383 ff.). The value of such a passage cannot be analysed: it can only be said that given such a subject, this alone is the right method of treatment.

Hesiod's diction is in the main Homeric, but one of his charms is the use of quaint allusive phrases derived, perhaps, from a pre-Hesiodic peasant poetry: thus the season when Boreas blows is the time when 'the Boneless One gnaws his foot by his fireless hearth in his cheerless house'; to cut one's nails is 'to sever the withered from the quick upon that which has five branches'; similarly the burglar is the 'day-sleeper', and the serpent is the 'hairless one'. Very similar is his reference to seasons through what happens or is done in that season: 'when the House-carrier, fleeing the Pleiades, climbs up the plants from the earth', is the season for harvesting; or 'when the artichoke flowers and the clicking grass-hopper, seated in a tree, pours down his shrill song', is the time for rest.

Hesiod's charm lies in his child-like and sincere naïveté, in his unaffected interest in and picturesque view of nature and all that happens in nature. These qualities, it is true, are those pre-eminently of the *Works and Days*: the literary values of the *Theogony* are of a more technical character, skill in ordering and disposing long lists of names, sure judgment in seasoning a monotonous subject with marvellous incidents or episodes, and no mean imagination in depicting the awful, as is shown in the description of Tartarus (ll. 736-745). Yet it remains true that Hesiod's distinctive title to a high place in Greek literature lies in the very fact of his freedom from classic form, and his grave, and yet child-like, outlook upon his world.

ENDNOTES

1. *sc. in Boeotia, Locris and Thessaly: elsewhere the movement was forced and unfruitful.*

2. *The extant collection of three poems, Works and Days, Theogony, and Shield of Heracles, which alone have come down to us complete, dates at least from the 4th century A.D.: the title of the Paris Papyrus (Bibl. Nat. Suppl. Gr. 1099) names only these three works.*

3. *Der Dialekt des Hesiodes, p. 464: examples are αὔνημι (W. and D. 683) and ἀρώμεναι (ib. 22).*

4. *T.W. Allen suggests that the conjured Delian and Pythian hymns to Apollo (Homeric Hymns III) may have suggested this version of the story, the Pythian hymn showing strong continental influence.*

5. *She is said to have given birth to the lyrist Stesichorus.*

6. *See Kinkel Epic. Graec. Frag. i. 158 ff.*

7. *See Great Works, frag. 2.*

8. *Hesiodi Fragmenta, pp. 119 f.*

9. Possibly the division of this poem into two books is a division belonging solely to this 'developed poem', which may have included in its second part a summary of the Tale of Troy.

10. Goettling's explanation.

11. x. 1. 52.

Zeus, Father of the Gods

Zeus and Thetis. Jean Ingres (1811)

THE THEOGONY OF HESIOD

(ll. 1-25) From the Heliconian Muses let us begin to sing, who hold the great and holy mount of Helicon, and dance on soft feet about the deep-blue spring and the altar of the almighty son of Cronos, and, when they have washed their tender bodies in Permessus or in the Horse's Spring or Olmeius, make their fair, lovely dances upon highest Helicon and move with vigorous feet. Thence they arise and go abroad by night, veiled in thick mist, and utter their song with lovely voice, praising Zeus the aegis-holder and queenly Hera of Argos who walks on golden sandals and the daughter of Zeus the aegis-holder bright-eyed Athene, and Phoebus Apollo, and Artemis who delights in arrows, and Poseidon the earth-holder who shakes the earth, and reverend Themis and quick-glancing[1] Aphrodite, and Hebe with the crown of gold, and fair Dione, Leto, Iapetus, and Cronos the crafty counsellor, Eos and great Helius and bright Selene, Earth too, and great Oceanus, and dark Night, and the holy race of all the other deathless ones that are for ever. And one day they taught Hesiod glorious song while he was shepherding his lambs under holy Helicon, and this word first the goddesses said to me – the Muses of Olympus, daughters of Zeus who holds the aegis:

(ll. 26-28) 'Shepherds of the wilderness, wretched things of shame, mere bellies, we know how to speak many false things as though they were true; but we know, when we will, to utter true things.'

(ll. 29-35) So said the ready-voiced daughters of great Zeus, and they plucked and gave me a rod, a shoot of sturdy laurel, a marvellous thing, and breathed into me a divine voice to celebrate things that shall be and things there were aforetime; and they bade me sing of the race of the blessed gods that are eternally, but ever to sing of themselves both first and last. But why all this about oak or stone?[2]

(ll. 36-52) Come thou, let us begin with the Muses who gladden the great spirit of their father Zeus in Olympus with their songs, telling of things that are and that shall be and that were aforetime with consenting voice. Unwearying flows the sweet sound from their lips, and the house of their father Zeus the loud-thunderer is glad at the lily-like voice of the goddesses as it spread abroad, and the peaks of snowy Olympus resound, and the homes of the immortals. And they uttering their immortal voice, celebrate in song first of all the reverend race of the gods from the beginning, those whom Earth and wide Heaven begot, and the gods sprung of these, givers of good things. Then, next, the goddesses sing of Zeus, the father of gods and men, as they begin and end their strain, how much he is the most excellent among the gods and supreme in power. And again, they chant the race of men and strong giants, and gladden the heart of Zeus within Olympus, – the Olympian Muses, daughters of Zeus the aegis-holder.

(ll. 53-74) Them in Pieria did Mnemosyne (Memory), who reigns over the hills of Eleuther, bear of union with the father, the son of Cronos, a forgetting of ills and a rest from sorrow. For nine nights did wise Zeus lie with her, entering her holy bed remote from the immortals. And when a year was passed and the seasons came round as the months waned, and many days were accomplished, she bare nine daughters, all of one mind, whose hearts are set upon song and their spirit free from care, a little way from the topmost peak of snowy Olympus. There are their bright dancing-places and beautiful homes, and beside them the Graces and Himerus (Desire) live in delight. And they, uttering through their lips a lovely voice, sing the laws of all and the goodly ways of the immortals, uttering their lovely voice. Then went they to Olympus, delighting in their sweet voice, with heavenly song, and the dark earth resounded about them as they chanted, and a lovely sound rose up beneath their feet as they went to their father. And he was reigning in heaven, himself holding the lightning and glowing thunderbolt, when he had overcome by might his father Cronos; and he distributed fairly to the immortals their portions and declared their privileges.

(ll. 75-103) These things, then, the Muses sang who dwell on Olympus, nine daughters begotten by great Zeus, Cleio and Euterpe, Thaleia, Melpomene and Terpsichore, and Erato and Polyhymnia and Urania and Calliope[3], who is the chiefest of them all, for she attends on worshipful princes: whomsoever of heaven-nourished princes the daughters of great Zeus honour, and behold him at his birth, they pour sweet dew upon his tongue, and from his lips flow gracious words. All the people look towards him while he settles causes with true judgements: and he, speaking surely, would soon make wise end even of a great quarrel; for therefore are there princes wise in heart, because when the people are being misguided in their assembly, they set right the matter again with ease, persuading them with gentle words. And when he passes through a gathering, they greet him as a god with gentle reverence, and he is conspicuous amongst the assembled: such is the holy gift of the Muses to men. For it is through the Muses and far-shooting Apollo that there are singers and harpers upon the earth; but princes are of Zeus, and happy is he whom the Muses love: sweet flows speech from his mouth. For though a man have sorrow and grief in his newly-troubled soul and live in dread because his heart is distressed, yet, when a singer, the servant of the Muses, chants the glorious deeds of men of old and the blessed gods who inhabit Olympus, at once he forgets his heaviness and remembers not his sorrows at all; but the gifts of the goddesses soon turn him away from these.

(ll. 104-115) Hail, children of Zeus! Grant lovely song and celebrate the holy race of the deathless gods who are for ever, those that were born of Earth and starry Heaven and gloomy Night and them that briny Sea did rear. Tell how at the first gods and earth came to be, and rivers, and the boundless sea with its raging swell, and the gleaming stars, and the wide heaven above, and the gods who were born of them, givers of good things, and how they divided their wealth, and how they shared their honours amongst them, and also how at the first they took many-folded Olympus. These things declare to me from the beginning, ye Muses who dwell in the house of Olympus, and tell me which of them first came to be.

(ll. 116-138) Verily at the first Chaos came to be, but next wide-bosomed Earth, the ever-sure foundations of all [4] the deathless ones who hold the peaks of snowy Olympus, and dim Tartarus in the depth of the wide-pathed Earth, and Eros (Love), fairest among the deathless gods, who unnerves the limbs and overcomes the mind and wise counsels of all gods and all men within them. From Chaos came forth Erebus and black Night; but of Night were born Aether[5] and Day, whom she conceived and bare from union in love with Erebus. And Earth first bare starry Heaven, equal to herself, to cover her on every side, and to be an ever-sure abiding-place for the blessed gods. And she brought forth long Hills, graceful haunts of the goddess-Nymphs who dwell amongst the glens of the hills. She bare also the fruitless deep with his raging swell, Pontus, without sweet union of love. But afterwards she lay with Heaven and bare deep-swirling Oceanus, Coeus and Crius and Hyperion and Iapetus, Theia and Rhea, Themis and Mnemosyne and gold-crowned Phoebe and lovely Tethys. After them was born Cronos the wily, youngest and most terrible of her children, and he hated his lusty sire.

(ll. 139-146) And again, she bare the Cyclopes, overbearing in spirit, Brontes, and Steropes and stubborn-hearted Arges[6], who gave Zeus the thunder and made the thunderbolt: in all else they were like the gods, but one eye only was set in the midst of their fore-heads. And they were surnamed Cyclopes (Orb-eyed) because one orbed eye was set in their foreheads. Strength and might and craft were in their works.

(ll. 147-163) And again, three other sons were born of Earth and Heaven, great and doughty beyond telling, Cottus and Briareos and Gyes, presumptuous children. From their shoulders sprang an hundred arms, not to be approached, and each had fifty heads upon his shoulders on their strong limbs, and irresistible was the stubborn strength that was in their great forms. For of all the children that were born of Earth and Heaven, these were the most terrible, and they were hated by their own father from the first.

And he used to hide them all away in a secret place of Earth so soon as each was born, and would not suffer them to come up into the light: and Heaven rejoiced in his evil doing. But vast Earth groaned within, being straitened, and she made the element of grey flint and shaped a great sickle, and told her plan to her dear sons. And she spoke, cheering them, while she was vexed in her dear heart:

(ll. 164-166) `My children, gotten of a sinful father, if you will obey me, we should punish the vile outrage of your father; for he first thought of doing shameful things.'

(ll. 167-169) So she said; but fear seized them all, and none of them uttered a word. But great Cronos the wily took courage and answered his dear mother:

(ll. 170-172) `Mother, I will undertake to do this deed, for I reverence not our father of evil name, for he first thought of doing shameful things.'

(ll. 173-175) So he said: and vast Earth rejoiced greatly in spirit, and set and hid him in an ambush, and put in his hands a jagged sickle, and revealed to him the whole plot.

(ll. 176-206) And Heaven came, bringing on night and longing for love, and he lay about Earth spreading himself full upon her[7].

Then the son from his ambush stretched forth his left hand and in his right took the great long sickle with jagged teeth, and swiftly lopped off his own father's members and cast them away to fall behind him. And not vainly did they fall from his hand; for all the bloody drops that gushed forth Earth received, and as the seasons moved round she bare the strong Erinyes and the great Giants with gleaming armour, holding long spears in their hands and the Nymphs whom they call Meliae[8] all over the boundless earth. And so soon as he had cut off the members with flint and cast them from the land into the surging sea, they were swept away over the main a long time: and a white foam spread around them from the immortal flesh, and in it there grew a maiden. First she drew near holy Cythera, and from there, afterwards, she came to sea-girt Cyprus, and came forth an awful and lovely goddess, and grass grew up about her beneath her shapely feet. Her gods and men call Aphrodite, and the foam-born goddess and rich-crowned Cytherea, because she grew amid the foam, and Cytherea because she reached Cythera, and Cyprogenes because she was born in billowy Cyprus, and Philommedes[9] because sprang from the members. And with her went Eros, and comely Desire followed her at her birth at the first and as she went into the assembly of the gods. This honour she has from the beginning, and this is the portion allotted to her amongst men and undying gods, – the whisperings of maidens and smiles and deceits with sweet delight and love and graciousness.

(ll. 207-210) But these sons whom he begot himself great Heaven used to call Titans (Strainers) in reproach, for he said that they strained and did presumptuously a fearful deed, and that vengeance for it would come afterwards.

(ll. 211-225) And Night bare hateful Doom and black Fate and Death, and she bare Sleep and the tribe of Dreams. And again the goddess murky Night, though she lay with none, bare Blame and painful Woe, and the Hesperides who guard the rich, golden apples and the trees bearing fruit beyond glorious Ocean. Also she bare the Destinies and ruthless avenging Fates, Clotho and Lachesis and Atropos[10], who give men at their birth both evil and good to have, and they pursue the transgressions of men and of gods: and these goddesses never cease from their dread anger until they punish the sinner with a sore penalty. Also deadly Night bare Nemesis (Indignation) to afflict mortal men, and after her, Deceit and Friendship and hateful Age and hard-hearted Strife.

(ll. 226-232) But abhorred Strife bare painful Toil and Forgetfulness and Famine and tearful Sorrows, Fightings also, Battles, Murders, Manslaughters, Quarrels, Lying Words, Disputes, Lawlessness and Ruin, all of one nature, and Oath who most troubles men upon earth when anyone wilfully swears a false oath.

(ll. 233-239) And Sea begat Nereus, the eldest of his children, who is true and lies not: and men call him the Old Man because he is trusty and gentle and does not forget the laws of righteousness, but thinks just and kindly thoughts. And yet again he got great Thaumas and proud Phoreys, being mated with Earth, and fair-cheeked Ceto and Eurybia who has a heart of flint within her.

(ll. 240-264) And of Nereus and rich-haired Doris, daughter of Ocean the perfect river, were born children[11], passing lovely amongst goddesses, Ploto, Eucrante, Sao, and Amphitrite, and Eudora, and Thetis, Galene and Glauce, Cymothoe, Speo, Thoe and lovely Halie, and Pasithea, and Erato, and rosy-armed Eunice, and gracious Melite, and Eulimene, and Agaue, Doto, Proto, Pherusa, and Dynamene, and Nisaea, and Actaea, and Protomedea, Doris, Panopea, and comely Galatea, and lovely Hippothoë, and rosy-armed Hipponoe, and Cymodoce who with Cymatolege[12] and Amphitrite easily calms the waves upon the misty sea and the blasts of raging winds, and Cymo, and Eione, and rich-crowned Alimede, and Glauconome, fond of laughter, and Pontoporea, Leagore, Euagore, and Laomedea, and Polynoë, and Autonoë, and Lysianassa, and Euarne, lovely of shape and without blemish of form, and Psamathe of charming figure and divine Menippe, Neso, Eupompe, Themisto, Pronoë, and Nemertes[13] who has the nature of her deathless father. These fifty daughters sprang from blameless Nereus, skilled in excellent crafts.

(ll. 265-269) And Thaumas wedded Electra the daughter of deep-flowing Ocean, and she bare him swift Iris and the long-haired Harpies, Aello (Storm-swift) and Ocypetes (Swift-flier) who on their swift wings keep pace with the blasts of the winds and the birds; for quick as time they dart along.

(ll 270-294) And again, Ceto bare to Phoreys the fair-cheeked Graiae, sisters grey from their birth: and both deathless gods and men who walk on earth call them Graiae, Pemphredo well-clad, and saffron-robed Enyo, and the Gorgons who dwell beyond glorious Ocean in the frontier land towards Night where are the clear-voiced Hesperides, Sthenno, and Euryale, and Medusa who suffered a woeful fate: she was mortal, but the two were undying and grew not old. With her lay the Dark-haired One[14] in a soft meadow amid spring flowers. And when Perseus cut off her head, there sprang forth great Chrysaor and the horse Pegasus who is so called because he was born near the springs (pegae) of Ocean; and that other, because he held a golden blade (aor) in his hands. Now Pegasus flew away and left the earth, the mother of flocks, and came to the deathless gods: and he dwells in the house of Zeus and brings to wise Zeus the thunder and lightning. But Chrysaor was joined in love to Callirrhoe, the daughter of glorious Ocean, and begot three-headed Geryones. Him mighty Heracles slew in sea-girt Erythea by his shambling oxen on that day when he drove the wide-browed oxen to holy Tiryns, and had crossed the ford of Ocean and killed Orthus and Eurytion the herdsman in the dim stead out beyond glorious Ocean.

(ll. 295-305) And in a hollow cave she bare another monster, irresistible, in no wise like either to mortal men or to the undying gods, even the goddess fierce Echidna who is half a nymph with glancing eyes and fair cheeks, and half again a huge snake, great and awful, with speckled skin, eating raw flesh beneath the secret parts of the holy earth. And there she has a cave deep down under a hollow rock far from the deathless gods and mortal men. There, then, did the gods appoint her a glorious house to dwell in: and she keeps guard in Arima beneath the earth, grim Echidna, a nymph who dies not nor grows old all her days.

(ll. 306-332) Men say that Typhaon the terrible, outrageous and lawless, was joined in love to her, the maid with glancing eyes. So she conceived and brought forth fierce offspring; first she bare Orthus the hound of Geryones, and then again she bare a second, a monster not to be overcome and that may not be described, Cerberus who eats raw flesh, the brazen-voiced hound of Hades, fifty-headed, relentless and strong. And again she bore a third, the evil-minded Hydra of Lerna, whom the goddess, white-armed Hera nourished, being angry beyond measure with the mighty Heracles. And her Heracles, the son of Zeus, of the house of Amphitryon, together with warlike Iolaus, destroyed with the unpitying sword through the plans of Athene the spoil-driver. She was the mother of Chimaera who breathed raging fire, a creature fearful, great, swift-footed and strong, who had three heads, one of a grim-eyed lion; in her hinderpart, a dragon; and in her middle, a goat, breathing forth a fearful blast of blazing fire. Her did Pegasus and noble Bellerophon slay; but Echidna was subject in love to Orthus and brought forth the deadly Sphinx which destroyed the Cadmeans, and the Nemean lion, which Hera, the good wife of Zeus, brought up and made to haunt the hills of Nemea, a plague to men. There he preyed upon the tribes of her own people and had power over Tretus of Nemea and Apesas: yet the strength of stout Heracles overcame him.

(ll. 333-336) And Ceto was joined in love to Phorcys and bare her youngest, the awful snake who guards the apples all of gold in the secret places of the dark earth at its great bounds. This is the offspring of Ceto and Phoreys.

(ll. 334-345) And Tethys bare to Ocean eddying rivers, Nilus, and Alpheus, and deep-swirling Eridanus, Strymon, and Meander, and the fair stream of Ister, and Phasis, and Rhesus, and the silver eddies of Achelous, Nessus, and Rhodius, Haliacmon, and

Heptaporus, Granicus, and Aesepus, and holy Simois, and Peneus, and Hermus, and Caicus fair stream, and great Sangarius, Ladon, Parthenius, Euenus, Ardescus, and divine Scamander.

(ll. 346-370) Also she brought forth a holy company of daughters[15] who with the lord Apollo and the Rivers have youths in their keeping – to this charge Zeus appointed them – Peitho, and Admete, and Ianthe, and Electra, and Doris, and Prymno, and Urania divine in form, Hippo, Clymene, Rhodea, and Callirrhoe, Zeuxo and Clytie, and Idyia, and Pasithoe, Plexaura, and Galaxaura, and lovely Dione, Melobosis and Thoe and handsome Polydora, Cerceis lovely of form, and soft eyed Pluto, Perseis, Ianeira, Acaste, Xanthe, Petraea the fair, Menestho, and Europa, Metis, and Eurynome, and Telesto saffron-clad, Chryseis and Asia and charming Calypso, Eudora, and Tyche, Amphirho, and Ocyrrhoe, and Styx who is the chiefest of them all. These are the eldest daughters that sprang from Ocean and Tethys; but there are many besides. For there are three thousand neat-ankled daughters of Ocean who are dispersed far and wide, and in every place alike serve the earth and the deep waters, children who are glorious among goddesses. And as many other rivers are there, babbling as they flow, sons of Ocean, whom queenly Tethys bare, but their names it is hard for a mortal man to tell, but people know those by which they severally dwell.

(ll. 371-374) And Theia was subject in love to Hyperion and bare great Helius (Sun) and clear Selene (Moon) and Eos (Dawn) who shines upon all that are on earth and upon the deathless Gods who live in the wide heaven.

(ll. 375-377) And Eurybia, bright goddess, was joined in love to Crius and bare great Astraeus, and Pallas, and Perses who also was eminent among all men in wisdom.

(ll. 378-382) And Eos bare to Astraeus the strong-hearted winds, brightening Zephyrus, and Boreas, headlong in his course, and Notus, – a goddess mating in love with a god. And after these Erigenia[16] bare the star Eosphorus (Dawn-bringer), and the gleaming stars with which heaven is crowned.

(ll. 383-403) And Styx the daughter of Ocean was joined to Pallas and bare Zelus (Emulation) and trim-ankled Nike (Victory) in the house. Also she brought forth Cratos (Strength) and Bia (Force), wonderful children. These have no house apart from Zeus, nor any dwelling nor path except that wherein God leads them, but they dwell always with Zeus the loud-thunderer. For so did Styx the deathless daughter of Ocean plan on that day when the Olympian Lightener called all the deathless gods to great Olympus, and said that whosoever of the gods would fight with him against the Titans, he would not cast him out from his rights, but each should have the office which he had before amongst the deathless gods. And he declared that he who was without office and rights under Cronos, should be raised to both office and rights as is just. So deathless Styx came first to Olympus with her children through the wit of her dear father. And Zeus honoured her, and gave her very great gifts, for her he appointed to be the great oath of the gods, and her children to live with him always. And as he promised, so he performed fully unto them all.

But he himself mightily reigns and rules.

(ll. 404-452) Again, Phoebe came to the desired embrace of Coeus. Then the goddess through the love of the god conceived and brought forth dark-gowned Leto, always mild, kind to men and to the deathless gods, mild from the beginning, gentlest in all Olympus. Also she bare Asteria of happy name, whom Perses once led to his great house to be called his dear wife. And she conceived and bare Hecate whom Zeus the son of Cronos honoured above all. He gave her splendid gifts, to have a share of the earth and the unfruitful sea. She received honour also in starry heaven, and is honoured exceedingly by the deathless gods. For to this day, whenever any one of men on earth offers rich sacrifices and prays for favour according to custom, he calls upon Hecate. Great honour comes full easily to him whose prayers the goddess receives favourably, and she bestows wealth upon him; for the power surely is with her. For as many as were born of Earth and Ocean amongst all these she has her due portion. The son of Cronos did her no wrong nor took anything away of all that was her portion among the former Titan gods: but she holds, as the division was at the first from the beginning, privilege both in earth, and in heaven, and in sea. Also, because she is an only child, the goddess receives not less honour, but much more still, for Zeus honours her. Whom she will she greatly aids and advances: she sits by worshipful kings in judgement, and in the assembly whom she will is distinguished among the people. And when men arm themselves for the battle that destroys men, then the goddess is at hand to give victory and grant glory readily to whom she will. Good is she also when men contend at the games, for there too the goddess is with them and profits them: and he who by might and strength gets the victory wins the rich prize easily with joy, and brings glory to his parents. And she is good to stand by horsemen, whom she will: and to those whose business is in the grey discomfortable sea, and who pray to Hecate and the loud-crashing Earth-Shaker, easily the glorious goddess gives great catch, and easily she takes it away as soon as seen, if so she will. She is good in the byre with Hermes to increase the stock. The droves of kine and wide herds of goats and flocks of fleecy sheep, if she will, she increases from a few, or makes many to be less. So, then. albeit her mother's only child [17], she is honoured amongst all the deathless gods. And the son of Cronos made her a nurse of the young who after that day saw with their eyes the light of all-seeing Dawn. So from the beginning she is a nurse of the young, and these are her honours.

(ll. 453-491) But Rhea was subject in love to Cronos and bare splendid children, Hestia[18], Demeter, and gold-shod Hera and strong Hades, pitiless in heart, who dwells under the earth, and the loud-crashing Earth-Shaker, and wise Zeus, father of gods and men, by whose thunder the wide earth is shaken. These great Cronos swallowed as each came forth from the womb to his mother's knees with this intent, that no other of the proud sons of Heaven should hold the kingly office amongst the deathless gods. For he learned from Earth and starry Heaven that he was destined to be overcome by his own son, strong though he was, through the contriving of great Zeus[19]. Therefore he kept no blind outlook, but watched and swallowed down his children: and unceasing grief seized Rhea. But when she was about to bear Zeus, the father of gods and men, then she besought her own dear parents, Earth and starry Heaven, to devise some plan with her that the birth of her dear child might be concealed, and that retribution might overtake great, crafty Cronos for his own father and also for the children whom he had swallowed down. And they readily heard and obeyed their dear daughter, and told her all that was destined to happen touching Cronos the king and his stout-hearted son. So they sent her to Lyetus, to the rich land of Crete, when she was ready to bear great Zeus, the youngest of her children. Him did vast Earth receive from Rhea in wide Crete to nourish and to bring up. Thither came Earth carrying him swiftly through the black night to Lyctus first, and took him in her arms and hid him in a remote cave beneath the secret places of the holy earth on thick-wooded Mount Aegeum; but to the mightily ruling son of Heaven, the earlier king of the gods, she gave a great stone wrapped in swaddling clothes. Then he took it in his hands and thrust it down into his belly: wretch! he knew not in his heart that in place of the stone his son was left behind, unconquered and untroubled, and that he was soon to overcome him by force and might and drive him from his honours, himself to reign over the deathless gods.

(ll. 492-506) After that, the strength and glorious limbs of the prince increased quickly, and as the years rolled on, great Cronos the wily was beguiled by the deep suggestions of Earth, and brought up again his offspring, vanquished by the arts and might of his own son, and he vomited up first the stone which he had swallowed last. And Zeus set it fast in the wide-pathed earth at goodly Pytho under the glens of Parnassus, to be a sign thenceforth and a marvel to mortal men[20]. And he set free from their deadly bonds the brothers of his father, sons of Heaven whom his father in his foolishness had bound. And they remembered to be grateful to him for his kindness, and gave him thunder and the glowing thunderbolt and lightening: for before that, huge Earth had hidden these. In them he trusts and rules over mortals and immortals.

(ll. 507-543) Now Iapetus took to wife the neat-ankled maid Clymene, daughter of Ocean, and went up with her into one bed. And she bare him a stout-hearted son, Atlas: also she bare very glorious Menoetius and clever Prometheus, full of various wiles, and scatter-brained Epimetheus who from the first was a mischief to men who eat bread; for it was he who first took of Zeus the woman, the maiden whom he had formed. But Menoetius was outrageous, and far-seeing Zeus struck him with a lurid thunderbolt and sent him down to Erebus because of his mad presumption and exceeding pride. And Atlas through hard constraint upholds the wide heaven with unwearying head and arms, standing at the borders of the earth before the clear-voiced Hesperides; for this lot wise Zeus assigned to him. And ready-witted Prometheus he bound with inextricable bonds, cruel chains, and drove a shaft through his middle, and set on him a long-winged eagle, which used to eat his immortal liver; but by night the liver grew as much again everyway as the long-winged bird devoured in the whole day. That bird Heracles, the valiant son of shapely-ankled Alcmene, slew; and delivered the son of Iapetus from the cruel plague, and released him from his affliction – not without the will of Olympian Zeus who reigns on high, that the glory of Heracles the Theban-born might be yet greater than it was before over the plenteous earth. This, then, he regarded, and honoured his famous son; though he was angry, he ceased from the wrath which he had before because Prometheus matched himself in wit with the almighty son of Cronos. For when the gods and mortal men had a dispute at Mecone, even then Prometheus was forward to cut up a great ox and set portions before them, trying to befool the mind of Zeus. Before the rest he set flesh and inner parts thick with fat upon the hide, covering them with an ox paunch; but for Zeus he put the white bones dressed up with cunning art and covered with shining fat. Then the father of men and of gods said to him:

(ll. 543-544) 'Son of Iapetus, most glorious of all lords, good sir, how unfairly you have divided the portions!'

(ll. 545-547) So said Zeus whose wisdom is everlasting, rebuking him. But wily Prometheus answered him, smiling softly and not forgetting his cunning trick:

(ll. 548-558) 'Zeus, most glorious and greatest of the eternal gods, take which ever of these portions your heart within you bids.' So he said, thinking trickery. But Zeus, whose wisdom is everlasting, saw and failed not to perceive the trick, and in his heart he thought mischief against mortal men which also was to be fulfilled. With both hands he took up the white fat and was angry at heart, and wrath came to his spirit when he saw the white ox-bones craftily tricked out: and because of this the tribes of men upon earth burn white bones to the deathless gods upon fragrant altars. But Zeus who drives the clouds was greatly vexed and said to him:

(ll. 559-560) 'Son of Iapetus, clever above all! So, sir, you have not yet forgotten your cunning arts!'

(ll. 561-584) So spake Zeus in anger, whose wisdom is everlasting; and from that time he was always mindful of the trick, and would not give the power of unwearying fire to the Melian[21] race of mortal men who live on the earth. But the noble son of Iapetus outwitted him and stole the far-seen gleam of unwearying fire in a hollow fennel stalk. And Zeus who thunders on high was stung in spirit, and his dear heart was angered when he saw amongst men the far-seen ray of fire. Forthwith he made an evil thing for men as the price of fire; for the very famous Limping God formed of earth the likeness of a shy maiden as the son of Cronos willed. And the goddess bright-eyed Athene girded and clothed her with silvery raiment, and down from her head she spread with her hands a broidered veil, a wonder to see; and she, Pallas Athene, put about her head lovely garlands, flowers of new-grown herbs. Also she put upon her head a crown of gold which the very famous Limping God made himself and worked with his own hands as a favour to Zeus his father. On it was much curious work, wonderful to see; for of the many creatures which the land and sea rear up, he put most upon it, wonderful things, like living beings with voices: and great beauty shone out from it.

(ll. 585-589) But when he had made the beautiful evil to be the price for the blessing, he brought her out, delighting in the finery which the bright-eyed daughter of a mighty father had given her, to the place where the other gods and men were. And wonder took hold of the deathless gods and mortal men when they saw that which was sheer guile, not to be withstood by men.

(ll. 590-612) For from her is the race of women and female kind: of her is the deadly race and tribe of women who live amongst mortal men to their great trouble, no helpmeets in hateful poverty, but only in wealth. And as in thatched hives bees feed the drones whose nature is to do mischief – by day and throughout the day until the sun goes down the bees are busy and lay the white combs, while the drones stay at home in the covered skeps and reap the toil of others into their own bellies – even so Zeus who thunders on high made women to be an evil to mortal men, with a nature to do evil. And he gave them a second evil to be the price for the good they had: whoever avoids marriage and the sorrows that women cause, and will not wed, reaches deadly old age without anyone to tend his years, and though he at least has no lack of livelihood while he lives, yet, when he is dead, his kinsfolk divide his possessions amongst them. And as for the man who chooses the lot of marriage and takes a good wife suited to his mind, evil continually contends with good; for whoever happens to have mischievous children, lives always with unceasing grief in his spirit and heart within him; and this evil cannot be healed.

(ll. 613-616) So it is not possible to deceive or go beyond the will of Zeus; for not even the son of Iapetus, kindly Prometheus, escaped his heavy anger, but of necessity strong bands confined him, although he knew many a wile.

(ll. 617-643) But when first their father was vexed in his heart with Obriareus and Cottus and Gyes, he bound them in cruel bonds, because he was jealous of their exceeding manhood and comeliness and great size: and he made them live beneath the wide-pathed earth, where they were afflicted, being set to dwell under the ground, at the end of the earth, at its great borders, in bitter anguish for a long time and with great grief at heart. But the son of Cronos and the other deathless gods whom rich-haired Rhea bare from union with Cronos, brought them up again to the light at Earth's advising. For she herself recounted all things to the gods fully, how that with these they would gain victory and a glorious cause to vaunt themselves. For the Titan gods and as many as sprang from Cronos had long been fighting together in stubborn war with heart-grieving toil, the lordly Titans from high Othyrs, but the gods, givers of good, whom rich-haired Rhea bare in union with Cronos, from Olympus. So they, with bitter wrath, were fighting continually with one another at that time for ten full years, and the hard strife had no close or end for either side, and the issue of the war hung evenly balanced. But when he had provided those three with all things fitting, nectar and ambrosia which the gods themselves eat, and when their proud spirit revived within them all after they had fed on nectar and delicious ambrosia, then it was that the father of men and gods spoke amongst them:

(ll. 644-653) 'Hear me, bright children of Earth and Heaven, that I may say what my heart within me bids. A long while now have we, who are sprung from Cronos and the Titan gods, fought with each other every day to get victory and to prevail. But do you show your great might and unconquerable strength, and face the Titans in bitter strife; for remember our friendly kindness, and from what sufferings you are come back to the light from your cruel bondage under misty gloom through our counsels.'

(ll. 654-663) So he said. And blameless Cottus answered him again: 'Divine one, you speak that which we know well: nay, even of ourselves we know that your wisdom and understanding is exceeding, and that you became a defender of the deathless ones from chill doom. And through your devising we are come back again from the murky gloom and from our merciless bonds, enjoying what we looked not for, O lord, son of Cronos. And so now with fixed purpose and deliberate counsel we will aid your power in dreadful strife and will fight against the Titans in hard battle.'

(ll. 664-686) So he said: and the gods, givers of good things, applauded when they heard his word, and their spirit longed for war even more than before, and they all, both male and female, stirred up hated battle that day, the Titan gods, and all that were born of Cronos together with those dread, mighty ones of overwhelming strength whom Zeus brought up to the light from Erebus beneath the earth. An hundred arms sprang from the shoulders of all alike, and each had fifty heads growing upon his shoulders upon stout limbs. These, then, stood against the Titans in grim strife, holding huge rocks in their strong hands. And on the other part the Titans eagerly strengthened their ranks, and both sides at one time showed the work of their hands and their might. The boundless sea rang terribly around, and the earth crashed loudly: wide Heaven was shaken and groaned, and high Olympus reeled from its foundation under the charge of the undying gods, and a heavy quaking reached dim Tartarus and the deep sound of their feet in the fearful onset and of their hard missiles. So, then, they launched their grievous shafts upon one another, and the cry of both armies as they shouted reached to starry heaven; and they met together with a great battle-cry.

(ll. 687-712) Then Zeus no longer held back his might; but straight his heart was filled with fury and he showed forth all his strength. From Heaven and from Olympus he came forthwith, hurling his lightning: the bolts flew thick and fast from his strong hand together with thunder and lightning, whirling an awesome flame. The life-giving earth crashed around in burning, and the vast wood crackled loud with fire all about. All the land seethed, and Ocean's streams and the unfruitful sea. The hot vapour lapped round the earthborn Titans: flame unspeakable rose to the bright upper air: the flashing glare of the thunder-stone and lightning blinded their eyes for all that they were strong. Astounding heat seized Chaos: and to see with eyes and to hear the sound with ears it seemed even as if Earth and wide Heaven above came together; for such a mighty crash would have arisen if Earth were being hurled to ruin, and Heaven from on high were hurling her down; so great a crash was there while the gods were meeting together in strife. Also the winds brought rumbling earthquake and duststorm, thunder and lightning and the lurid thunderbolt, which are the shafts of great Zeus, and carried the clangour and the war-cry into the midst of the two hosts. An horrible uproar of terrible strife arose: mighty deeds were shown and the battle inclined. But until then, they kept at one another and fought continually in cruel war.

(ll. 713-735) And amongst the foremost Cottus and Briareos and Gyes insatiate for war raised fierce fighting: three hundred rocks, one upon another, they launched from their strong hands and overshadowed the Titans with their missiles, and buried them beneath the wide-pathed earth, and bound them in bitter chains when they had conquered them by their strength for all their great spirit, as far beneath the earth to Tartarus. For a brazen anvil falling down from heaven nine nights and days would reach the earth upon the tenth: and again, a brazen anvil falling from earth nine nights and days would reach Tartarus upon the tenth. Round it runs a fence of bronze, and night spreads in triple line all about it like a neck-circlet, while above grow the roots of the earth and unfruitful sea. There by the counsel of Zeus who drives the clouds the Titan gods are hidden under misty gloom, in a dank place where are the ends of the huge earth. And they may not go out; for Poseidon fixed gates of bronze upon it, and a wall runs all round it on every side. There Gyes and Cottus and great-souled Obriareus live, trusty warders of Zeus who holds the aegis.

(ll. 736-744) And there, all in their order, are the sources and ends of gloomy earth and misty Tartarus and the unfruitful sea and starry heaven, loathsome and dank, which even the gods abhor.

It is a great gulf, and if once a man were within the gates, he would not reach the floor until a whole year had reached its end, but cruel blast upon blast would carry him this way and that. And this marvel is awful even to the deathless gods.

(ll. 744-757) There stands the awful home of murky Night wrapped in dark clouds. In front of it the son of Iapetus[22] stands immovably upholding the wide heaven upon his head and unwearying hands, where Night and Day draw near and greet one another as they pass the great threshold of bronze: and while the one is about to go down into the house, the other comes out at the door.

And the house never holds them both within; but always one is without the house passing over the earth, while the other stays at home and waits until the time for her journeying come; and the one holds all-seeing light for them on earth, but the other holds in her arms Sleep the brother of Death, even evil Night, wrapped in a vaporous cloud.

(ll. 758-766) And there the children of dark Night have their dwellings, Sleep and Death, awful gods. The glowing Sun never looks upon them with his beams, neither as he goes up into heaven, nor as he comes down from heaven. And the former of them roams peacefully over the earth and the sea's broad back and is kindly to men; but the other has a heart of iron, and his spirit within him is pitiless as bronze: whomsoever of men he has once seized he holds fast: and he is hateful even to the deathless gods.

(ll. 767-774) There, in front, stand the echoing halls of the god of the lower-world, strong Hades, and of awful Persephone. A fearful hound guards the house in front, pitiless, and he has a cruel trick. On those who go in he fawns with his tail and both his ears, but suffers them not to go out back again, but keeps watch and devours whomsoever he catches going out of the gates of strong Hades and awful Persephone.

(ll. 775-806) And there dwells the goddess loathed by the deathless gods, terrible Styx, eldest daughter of back-flowing[23] Ocean. She lives apart from the gods in her glorious house vaulted over with great rocks and propped up to heaven all round with silver pillars. Rarely does the daughter of Thaumas, swift- footed Iris, come to her with a message over the sea's wide back.

But when strife and quarrel arise among the deathless gods, and when any of them who live in the house of Olympus lies, then Zeus sends Iris to bring in a golden jug the great oath of the gods from far away, the famous cold water which trickles down from a high and beetling rock. Far under the wide-pathed earth a branch of Oceanus flows through the dark night out of the holy stream, and a tenth part of his water is allotted to her. With nine silver-swirling streams he winds about the earth and the sea's wide back, and then falls into the main[24]; but the tenth flows out from a rock, a sore trouble to the gods. For whoever of the deathless gods that hold the peaks of snowy Olympus pours a libation of her water is forsworn, lies breathless until a full year is completed, and never comes near to taste ambrosia and nectar, but lies spiritless and voiceless on a strewn bed: and a heavy trance overshadows him. But when he has spent a long year in his sickness, another penance and an harder follows after the first. For nine years he is cut off from the eternal gods and never joins their councils or their feasts, nine full years. But in the tenth year he comes again to join the assemblies of the deathless gods who live in the house of Olympus. Such an oath, then, did the gods appoint the eternal and primaeval water of Styx to be: and it spouts through a rugged place.

(ll. 807-819) And there, all in their order, are the sources and ends of the dark earth and misty Tartarus and the unfruitful sea and starry heaven, loathsome and dank, which even the gods abhor.

And there are shining gates and an immoveable threshold of bronze having unending roots and it is grown of itself[25]. And beyond, away from all the gods, live the Titans, beyond gloomy Chaos. But the glorious allies of loud-crashing Zeus have their dwelling upon Ocean's foundations, even Cottus and Gyes; but Briareos, being goodly, the deep-roaring Earth-Shaker made his son-in-law, giving him Cymopolea his daughter to wed.

(ll. 820-868) But when Zeus had driven the Titans from heaven, huge Earth bare her youngest child Typhoeus of the love of Tartarus, by the aid of golden Aphrodite. Strength was with his hands in all that he did and the feet of the strong god were untiring. From his shoulders grew an hundred heads of a snake, a fearful dragon, with dark, flickering tongues, and from under the brows of his eyes in his marvellous heads flashed fire, and fire burned from his heads as he glared. And there were voices in all his dreadful heads which uttered every kind of sound unspeakable; for at one time they made sounds such that the gods understood, but at another, the noise of a bull bellowing aloud in proud ungovernable fury; and at another, the sound of a lion, relentless of heart; and at anothers, sounds like whelps, wonderful to hear; and again, at another, he would hiss, so that the high mountains re-echoed. And truly a thing past help would have happened on that day, and he would have come to reign over mortals and immortals, had not the father of men and gods been quick to perceive it. But he thundered hard and mightily: and the earth around resounded terribly and the wide heaven above, and the sea and Ocean's streams and the nether parts of the earth. Great Olympus reeled beneath the divine feet of the king as he arose and earth groaned thereat. And through the two of them heat took hold on the dark-blue sea, through the thunder and lightning, and through the fire from the monster, and the scorching winds and blazing thunderbolt. The whole earth seethed, and sky and sea: and the long waves raged along the beaches round and about, at the rush of the deathless gods: and there arose an endless shaking. Hades trembled where he rules over the dead below, and the Titans under Tartarus who live with Cronos, because of the unending clamour and the fearful strife. So when Zeus had raised up his might and seized his arms, thunder and lightning and lurid thunderbolt, he leaped form Olympus and struck him, and burned all the marvellous heads of the monster about him. But when Zeus had conquered him and lashed him with strokes, Typhoeus was hurled down, a maimed wreck, so that the huge earth groaned. And flame shot forth from the thunder-stricken lord in the dim rugged glens of the mount[26], when he was smitten. A great part of huge earth was scorched by the terrible vapour and melted as tin melts when heated by men's art in channelled [27] crucibles; or as iron, which is hardest of all things, is softened by glowing fire in mountain glens and melts in the divine earth through the strength of Hephaestus[28]. Even so, then, the earth melted in the glow of the blazing fire. And in the bitterness of his anger Zeus cast him into wide Tartarus.

(ll. 869-880) And from Typhoeus come boisterous winds which blow damply, except Notus and Boreas and clear Zephyr. These are a god-sent kind, and a great blessing to men; but the others blow fitfully upon the seas. Some rush upon the misty sea and work great havoc among men with their evil, raging blasts; for varying with the season they blow, scattering ships and destroying sailors. And men who meet these upon the sea have no help against the mischief.

Others again over the boundless, flowering earth spoil the fair fields of men who dwell below, filling them with dust and cruel uproar.

(ll. 881-885) But when the blessed gods had finished their toil, and settled by force their struggle for honours with the Titans, they pressed far-seeing Olympian Zeus to reign and to rule over them, by Earth's prompting. So he divided their dignities amongst them.

(ll. 886-900) Now Zeus, king of the gods, made Metis his wife first, and she was wisest among gods and mortal men. But when she was about to bring forth the goddess bright-eyed Athene, Zeus craftily deceived her with cunning words and put her in his own belly, as Earth and starry Heaven advised. For they advised him so, to the end that no other should hold royal sway over the eternal gods in place of Zeus; for very wise children were destined to be born of her, first the maiden bright-eyed Tritogeneia, equal to her father in strength and in wise understanding; but afterwards she was to bear a son of overbearing spirit, king of gods and men. But Zeus put her into his own belly first, that the goddess might devise for him both good and evil.

(ll. 901-906) Next he married bright Themis who bare the Horae (Hours), and Eunomia (Order), Dike (Justice), and blooming Eirene (Peace), who mind the works of mortal men, and the Moerae (Fates) to whom wise Zeus gave the greatest honour, Clotho, and Lachesis, and Atropos who give mortal men evil and good to have.

(ll. 907-911) And Eurynome, the daughter of Ocean, beautiful in form, bare him three fair-cheeked Charites (Graces), Aglaea, and Euphrosyne, and lovely Thaleia, from whose eyes as they glanced flowed love that unnerves the limbs: and beautiful is their glance beneath their brows.

(ll. 912-914) Also he came to the bed of all-nourishing Demeter, and she bare white-armed Persephone whom Aidoneus carried off from her mother; but wise Zeus gave her to him.

(ll. 915-917) And again, he loved Mnemosyne with the beautiful hair: and of her the nine gold-crowned Muses were born who delight in feasts and the pleasures of song.

(ll. 918-920) And Leto was joined in love with Zeus who holds the aegis, and bare Apollo and Artemis delighting in arrows, children lovely above all the sons of Heaven.

(ll. 921-923) Lastly, he made Hera his blooming wife: and she was joined in love with the king of gods and men, and brought forth Hebe and Ares and Eileithyia.

(ll. 924-929) But Zeus himself gave birth from his own head to bright-eyed Tritogeneia[29], the awful, the strife-stirring, the host-leader, the unwearying, the queen, who delights in tumults and wars and battles. But Hera without union with Zeus – for she was very angry and quarrelled with her mate – bare famous Hephaestus, who is skilled in crafts more than all the sons of Heaven.

(ll. 929a-929t)[30] But Hera was very angry and quarrelled with her mate. And because of this strife she bare without union with Zeus who holds the aegis a glorious son, Hephaestus, who excelled all the sons of Heaven in crafts. But Zeus lay with the fair-cheeked daughter of Ocean and Tethys apart from Hera.... (LACUNA) ....deceiving Metis (Thought) although she was full wise. But he seized her with his hands and put her in his belly, for fear that she might bring forth something stronger than his thunderbolt: therefore did Zeus, who sits on high and dwells in the aether, swallow her down suddenly. But she straightway conceived Pallas Athene: and the father of men and gods gave her birth by way of his head on the banks of the river Trito. And she remained hidden beneath the inward parts of Zeus, even Metis, Athena's mother, worker of righteousness, who was wiser than gods and mortal men. There the goddess (Athena) received that [31] whereby she excelled in strength all the deathless ones who dwell in Olympus, she who made the host-scaring weapon of Athena. And with it (Zeus) gave her birth, arrayed in arms of war.

(ll. 930-933) And of Amphitrite and the loud-roaring Earth-Shaker was born great, wide-ruling Triton, and he owns the depths of the sea, living with his dear mother and the lord his father in their golden house, an awful god.

(ll. 933-937) Also Cytherea bare to Ares the shield-piercer Panic and Fear, terrible gods who drive in disorder the close ranks of men in numbing war, with the help of Ares, sacker of towns: and Harmonia whom high-spirited Cadmus made his wife.

(ll. 938-939) And Maia, the daughter of Atlas, bare to Zeus glorious Hermes, the herald of the deathless gods, for she went up into his holy bed.

(ll. 940-942) And Semele, daughter of Cadmus was joined with him in love and bare him a splendid son, joyous Dionysus, – a mortal woman an immortal son. And now they both are gods.

(ll. 943-944) And Alemena was joined in love with Zeus who drives the clouds and bare mighty Heracles.

(ll. 945-946) And Hephaestus, the famous Lame One, made Aglaea, youngest of the Graces, his buxom wife.

(ll. 947-949) And golden-haired Dionysus made brown-haired Ariadne, the daughter of Minos, his buxom wife: and the son of Cronos made her deathless and unageing for him.

(ll. 950-955) And mighty Heracles, the valiant son of neat-ankled Alemena, when he had finished his grievous toils, made Hebe the child of great Zeus and gold-shod Hera his shy wife in snowy Olympus. Happy he! For he has finished his great works and lives amongst the undying gods, untroubled and unageing all his days.

(ll. 956-962) And Perseis, the daughter of Ocean, bare to unwearying Helios Circe and Aeetes the king. And Aeetes, the son of Helios who shows light to men, took to wife fair-cheeked Idyia, daughter of Ocean the perfect stream, by the will of the gods: and she was subject to him in love through golden Aphrodite and bare him neat-ankled Medea.

(ll. 963-968) And now farewell, you dwellers on Olympus and you islands and continents and thou briny sea within. Now sing the company of goddesses, sweet-voiced Muses of Olympus, daughter of Zeus who holds the aegis, – even those deathless one who lay with mortal men and bare children like unto gods.

(ll. 969-974) Demeter, bright goddess, was joined in sweet love with the hero Iasion in a thrice-ploughed fallow in the rich land of Crete, and bare Plutus, a kindly god who goes everywhere over land and the sea's wide back, and him who finds him and into whose hands he comes he makes rich, bestowing great wealth upon him.

(ll. 975-978) And Harmonia, the daughter of golden Aphrodite, bare to Cadmus Ino and Semele and fair-cheeked Agave and Autonoe whom long-haired Aristaeus wedded, and Polydorus also in rich-crowned Thebe.

(ll. 979-983) And the daughter of Ocean, Callirrhoe was joined in the love of rich Aphrodite with stout hearted Chrysaor and bare a son who was the strongest of all men, Geryones, whom mighty Heracles killed in sea-girt Erythea for the sake of his shambling oxen.

(ll. 984-991) And Eos bare to Tithonus brazen-crested Memnon, king of the Ethiopians, and the Lord Emathion. And to Cephalus she bare a splendid son, strong Phaethon, a man like the gods, whom, when he was a young boy in the tender flower of glorious youth with childish thoughts, laughter-loving Aphrodite seized and caught up and made a keeper of her shrine by night, a divine spirit.

(ll. 993-1002) And the son of Aeson by the will of the gods led away from Aeetes the daughter of Aeetes the heaven-nurtured king, when he had finished the many grievous labours which the great king, over bearing Pelias, that outrageous and presumptuous doer of violence, put upon him. But when the son of Aeson had finished them, he came to Iolcus after long toil bringing the coy-eyed girl with him on his swift ship, and made her his buxom wife. And she was subject to Iason, shepherd of the people, and bare a son Medeus whom Cheiron the son of Philyra brought up in the mountains. And the will of great Zeus was fulfilled.

(ll. 1003-1007) But of the daughters of Nereus, the Old man of the Sea, Psamathe the fair goddess, was loved by Aeacus through golden Aphrodite and bare Phocus. And the silver-shod goddess Thetis was subject to Peleus and brought forth lion-hearted Achilles, the destroyer of men.

(ll. 1008-1010) And Cytherea with the beautiful crown was joined in sweet love with the hero Anchises and bare Aeneas on the peaks of Ida with its many wooded glens.

(ll. 1011-1016) And Circe the daughter of Helius, Hyperion's son, loved steadfast Odysseus and bare Agrius and Latinus who was faultless and strong: also she brought forth Telegonus by the will of golden Aphrodite. And they ruled over the famous Tyrenians, very far off in a recess of the holy islands.

(ll. 1017-1018) And the bright goddess Calypso was joined to Odysseus in sweet love, and bare him Nausithous and Nausinous.

(ll. 1019-1020) These are the immortal goddesses who lay with mortal men and bare them children like unto gods.

(ll. 1021-1022) But now, sweet-voiced Muses of Olympus, daughters of Zeus who holds the aegis, sing of the company of women.

ENDNOTES:

(1) The epithet probably indicates coquettishness.

(2) A proverbial saying meaning, `why enlarge on irrelevant topics?'

(3) `She of the noble voice': Calliope is queen of Epic poetry.

(4) Earth, in the cosmology of Hesiod, is a disk surrounded by the river Oceanus and floating upon a waste of waters. It is called the foundation of all (the qualification `the deathless ones...' etc. is an interpolation), because not only trees, men, and animals, but even the hills and seas (ll. 129, 131) are supported by it.

(5) Aether is the bright, untainted upper atmosphere, as distinguished from Aer, the lower atmosphere of the earth.

(6) Brontes is the Thunderer; Steropes, the Lightener; Arges, the Vivid One.

(7) The myth accounts for the separation of Heaven and Earth. In Egyptian cosmology Nut (the Sky) is thrust and held apart from her brother Geb (the Earth) by their father Shu, who corresponds to the Greek Atlas.

(8) Nymphs of the ash-trees, as Dryads are nymphs of the oak- trees. Cp. note on "Works and Days", l. 145.

(9) `Member-loving': the title is perhaps only a perversion of the regular Φιλομειδής (Philomeides – laughter-loving).

(10) Cletho (the Spinner) is she who spins the thread of man's life; Lachesis (the Disposer of Lots) assigns to each man his destiny; Atropos (She who cannot be turned) is the `Fury with the abhorred shears.'

(11) Many of the names which follow express various qualities or aspects of the sea: thus Galene is `Calm', Cymothoe is the `Wave-swift', Pherusa and Dynamene are `She who speeds (ships)' and `She who has power'.

(12) The `Wave-receiver' and the `Wave-stiller'.

(13) `The Unerring' or `Truthful'; cp. l. 235.

(14) i.e. Poseidon.

(15) Goettling notes that some of these nymphs derive their names from lands over which they preside, as Europa, Asia, Doris, Ianeira (`Lady of the Ionians'), but that most are called after some quality which their streams possessed: thus Xanthe is the `Brown' or `Turbid', Amphirho is the `Surrounding' river, Ianthe is `She who delights', and Ocyrrhoe is the `Swift-flowing'.

(16) i.e. Eos, the `Early-born'.

(17) Van Lennep explains that Hecate, having no brothers to support her claim, might have been slighted.

(18) The goddess of the hearth (the Roman "Vesta"), and so of the house. Cp. "Homeric Hymns" v.22 ff.; xxxix.1 ff.

(19) The variant reading 'of his father' (sc. Heaven) rests on inferior MS. authority and is probably an alteration due to the difficulty stated by a Scholiast: 'How could Zeus, being not yet begotten, plot against his father?' The phrase is, however, part of the prophecy. The whole line may well be spurious, and is rejected by Heyne, Wolf, Gaisford and Guyet.

(20) Pausanias (x. 24.6) saw near the tomb of Neoptolemus 'a stone of no great size', which the Delphians anointed every day with oil, and which he says was supposed to be the stone given to Cronos.

(21) A Scholiast explains: 'Either because they (men) sprang from the Melian nymphs (cp. l. 187); or because, when they were born (?), they cast themselves under the ash-trees, that is, the trees.' The reference may be to the origin of men from ash-trees: cp. "Works and Days", l. 145 and note.

(22) sc. Atlas, the Shu of Egyptian mythology.

(23) Oceanus is here regarded as a continuous stream enclosing the earth and the seas, and so as flowing back upon himself.

(24) The conception of Oceanus is here different: he has nine streams which encircle the earth and the flow out into the 'main' which appears to be the waste of waters on which, according to early Greek and Hebrew cosmology, the disk-like earth floated.

(25) i.e. the threshold is of 'native' metal, and not artificial.

(26) According to Homer Typhoeus was overwhelmed by Zeus amongst the Arimi in Cilicia. Pindar represents him as buried under Aetna, and Tzetzes reads Aetna in this passage.

(27) The epithet (which means literally 'well-bored') seems to refer to the spout of the crucible.

(28) The fire god. There is no reference to volcanic action: iron was smelted on Mount Ida; cp. "Epigrams of Homer", ix. 2-4.

(29) i.e. Athena, who was born 'on the banks of the river Trito' (cp. l. 929l)

(30) Restored by Peppmuller. The nineteen following lines from another recension of lines 889-900, 924-9 are quoted by Chrysippus (in Galen).

(31) sc. the aegis. Line 929s is probably spurious, since it disagrees with l.929q and contains a suspicious reference to Athens.

Seafaring and Viniculture
Attic Ware (c.500 BCE)

HESIOD: WORKS AND DAYS

(ll. 1-10) Muses of Pieria who give glory through song, come hither, tell of Zeus your father and chant his praise. Through him mortal men are famed or un-famed, sung or unsung alike, as great Zeus wills. For easily he makes strong, and easily he brings the strong man low; easily he humbles the proud and raises the obscure, and easily he straightens the crooked and blasts the proud, – Zeus who thunders aloft and has his dwelling most high.

Attend thou with eye and ear, and make judgements straight with righteousness. And I, Perses, would tell of true things.

(ll. 11-24) So, after all, there was not one kind of Strife alone, but all over the earth there are two. As for the one, a man would praise her when he came to understand her; but the other is blameworthy: and they are wholly different in nature. For one fosters evil war and battle, being cruel: her no man loves; but perforce, through the will of the deathless gods, men pay harsh Strife her honour due. But the other is the elder daughter of dark Night, and the son of Cronos who sits above and dwells in the aether, set her in the roots of the earth: and she is far kinder to men. She stirs up even the shiftless to toil; for a man grows eager to work when he considers his neighbour, a rich man who hastens to plough and plant and put his house in good order; and neighbour vies with is neighbour as he hurries after wealth. This Strife is wholesome for men. And potter is angry with potter, and craftsman with craftsman, and beggar is jealous of beggar, and minstrel of minstrel.

(ll. 25-41) Perses, lay up these things in your heart, and do not let that Strife who delights in mischief hold your heart back from work, while you peep and peer and listen to the wrangles of the court-house. Little concern has he with quarrels and courts who has not a year's victuals laid up betimes, even that which the earth bears, Demeter's grain. When you have got plenty of that, you can raise disputes and strive to get another's goods. But you shall have no second chance to deal so again: nay, let us settle our dispute here with true judgement which is of Zeus and is perfect. For we had already divided our inheritance, but you seized the greater share and carried it off, greatly swelling the glory of our bribe-swallowing lords who love to judge such a cause as this. Fools! They know not how much more the half is than the whole, nor what great advantage there is in mallow and asphodel[1].

(ll. 42-53) For the gods keep hidden from men the means of life. Else you would easily do work enough in a day to supply you for a full year even without working; soon would you put away your rudder over the smoke, and the fields worked by ox and sturdy mule would run to waste. But Zeus in the anger of his heart hid it, because Prometheus the crafty deceived him; therefore he planned sorrow and mischief against men. He hid fire; but that the noble son of Iapetus stole again for men from Zeus the counsellor in a hollow fennel-stalk, so that Zeus who delights in thunder did not see it. But afterwards Zeus who gathers the clouds said to him in anger:

(ll. 54-59) 'Son of Iapetus, surpassing all in cunning, you are glad that you have outwitted me and stolen fire – a great plague to you yourself and to men that shall be. But I will give men as the price for fire an evil thing in which they may all be glad of heart while they embrace their own destruction.'

(ll. 60-68) So said the father of men and gods, and laughed aloud. And he bade famous Hephaestus make haste and mix earth with water and to put in it the voice and strength of human kind, and fashion a sweet, lovely maiden-shape, like to the immortal goddesses in face; and Athene to teach her needlework and the weaving of the varied web; and golden Aphrodite to shed grace upon her head and cruel longing and cares that weary the limbs. And he charged Hermes the guide, the Slayer of Argus, to put in her a shameless mind and a deceitful nature.

(ll. 69-82) So he ordered. And they obeyed the lord Zeus the son of Cronos. Forthwith the famous Lame God moulded clay in the likeness of a modest maid, as the son of Cronos purposed. And the goddess bright-eyed Athene girded and clothed her, and the divine Graces and queenly Persuasion put necklaces of gold upon her, and the rich-haired Hours crowned her head with spring flowers. And Pallas Athene bedecked her form with all manners of finery. Also the Guide, the Slayer of Argus, contrived within her lies and crafty words and a deceitful nature at the will of loud thundering Zeus, and the Herald of the gods put speech in her. And he called this woman Pandora[2], because all they who dwelt on Olympus gave each a gift, a plague to men who eat bread.

(ll. 83-89) But when he had finished the sheer, hopeless snare, the Father sent glorious Argus-Slayer, the swift messenger of the gods, to take it to Epimetheus as a gift. And Epimetheus did not think on what Prometheus had said to him, bidding him never take a gift of Olympian Zeus, but to send it back for fear it might prove to be something harmful to men. But he took the gift, and afterwards, when the evil thing was already his, he understood.

(ll. 90-105) For ere this the tribes of men lived on earth remote and free from ills and hard toil and heavy sickness which bring the Fates upon men; for in misery men grow old quickly. But the woman took off the great lid of the jar[3] with her hands and scattered all these and her thought caused sorrow and mischief to men. Only Hope remained there in an unbreakable home within under the rim of the great jar, and did not fly out at the door; for ere that, the lid of the jar stopped her, by the will of Aegis-holding Zeus who gathers the clouds. But the rest, countless plagues, wander amongst men; for earth is full of evils and the sea is full. Of themselves diseases come upon men continually by day and by night, bringing mischief to mortals silently; for wise Zeus took away speech from them. So is there no way to escape the will of Zeus.

(ll. 106-108) Or if you will, I will sum you up another tale well and skilfully – and do you lay it up in your heart, – how the gods and mortal men sprang from one source.

(ll. 109-120) First of all the deathless gods who dwell on Olympus made a golden race of mortal men who lived in the time of Cronos when he was reigning in heaven. And they lived like gods without sorrow of heart, remote and free from toil and grief: miserable age rested not on them; but with legs and arms never failing they made merry with feasting beyond the reach of all evils. When they died, it was as though they were overcome with sleep, and they had all good things; for the fruitful earth unforced bare them fruit abundantly and without stint. They dwelt in ease and peace upon their lands with many good things, rich in flocks and loved by the blessed gods.

(ll. 121-139) But after earth had covered this generation – they are called pure spirits dwelling on the earth, and are kindly, delivering from harm, and guardians of mortal men; for they roam everywhere over the earth, clothed in mist and keep watch on judgements and cruel deeds, givers of wealth; for this royal right also they received; – then they who dwell on Olympus made a second generation which was of silver and less noble by far. It was like the golden race neither in body nor in spirit. A child was brought up at his good mother's side an hundred years, an utter simpleton, playing childishly in his own home. But when they were full grown and were come to the full measure of their prime, they lived only a little time in sorrow because of their foolishness, for they could not keep from sinning and from wronging one another, nor would they serve the immortals, nor sacrifice on the holy altars of the blessed ones as it is right for men to do wherever they dwell. Then Zeus the son of Cronos was angry and put them away, because they would not give honour to the blessed gods who live on Olympus.

(ll. 140-155) But when earth had covered this generation also

– they are called blessed spirits of the underworld by men, and, though they are of second order, yet honour attends them also – Zeus the Father made a third generation of mortal men, a brazen race, sprung from ash-trees [4]; and it was in no way equal to the silver age, but was terrible and strong. They loved the lamentable works of Ares and deeds of violence; they ate no bread, but were hard of heart like adamant, fearful men. Great was their strength and unconquerable the arms which grew from their shoulders on their strong limbs. Their armour was of bronze, and their houses of bronze, and of bronze were their implements: there was no black iron. These were destroyed by their own hands and passed to the dank house of chill Hades, and left no name: terrible though they were, black Death seized them, and they left the bright light of the sun.

(ll. 156-169b) But when earth had covered this generation also, Zeus the son of Cronos made yet another, the fourth, upon the fruitful earth, which was nobler and more righteous, a god-like race of hero-men who are called demi-gods, the race before our own, throughout the boundless earth. Grim war and dread battle destroyed a part of them, some in the land of Cadmus at seven-gated Thebe when they fought for the flocks of Oedipus, and some, when it had brought them in ships over the great sea gulf to Troy for rich-haired Helen's sake: there death's end enshrouded a part of them. But to the others father Zeus the son of Cronos gave a living and an abode apart from men, and made them dwell at the ends of earth. And they live untouched by sorrow in the islands of the blessed along the shore of deep swirling Ocean, happy heroes for whom the grain-giving earth bears honey-sweet fruit flourishing thrice a year, far from the deathless gods, and Cronos rules over them [5]; for the father of men and gods released him from his bonds. And these last equally have honour and glory.

(ll. 169c-169d) And again far-seeing Zeus made yet another generation, the fifth, of men who are upon the bounteous earth.

(ll. 170-201) Thereafter, would that I were not among the men of the fifth generation, but either had died before or been born afterwards. For now truly is a race of iron, and men never rest from labour and sorrow by day, and from perishing by night; and the gods shall lay sore trouble upon them. But, notwithstanding, even these shall have some good mingled with their evils. And Zeus will destroy this race of mortal men also when they come to have grey hair on the temples at their birth [6]. The father will not agree with his children, nor the children with their father, nor guest with his host, nor comrade with comrade; nor will brother be dear to brother as aforetime. Men will dishonour their parents as they grow quickly old, and will carp at them, chiding them with bitter words, hard-hearted they, not knowing the fear of the gods. They will not repay their aged parents the cost of their nurture, for might shall be their right: and one man will sack another's city. There will be no favour for the man who keeps his oath or for the just or for the good; but rather men will praise the evil-doer and his violent dealing. Strength will be right and reverence will cease to be; and the wicked will hurt the worthy man, speaking false words against him, and will swear an oath upon them. Envy, foul-mouthed, delighting in evil, with scowling face, will go along with wretched men one and all. And then Aidos and Nemesis[7], with their sweet forms wrapped in white robes, will go from the wide-pathed earth and forsake mankind to join the company of the deathless gods: and bitter sorrows will be left for mortal men, and there will be no help against evil.

(ll. 202-211) And now I will tell a fable for princes who themselves understand. Thus said the hawk to the nightingale with speckled neck, while he carried her high up among the clouds, gripped fast in his talons, and she, pierced by his crooked talons, cried pitifully. To her he spoke disdainfully: `Miserable thing, why do you cry out? One far stronger than you now holds you fast, and you must go wherever I take you, songstress as you are. And if I please I will make my meal of you, or let you go. He is a fool who tries to withstand the stronger, for he does not get the mastery and suffers pain besides his shame.' So said the swiftly flying hawk, the long-winged bird.

(ll. 212-224) But you, Perses, listen to right and do not foster violence; for violence is bad for a poor man. Even the prosperous cannot easily bear its burden, but is weighed down under it when he has fallen into delusion. The better path is to go by on the other side towards justice; for Justice beats Outrage when she comes at length to the end of the race. But only when he has suffered does the fool learn this. For Oath keeps pace with wrong judgements. There is a noise when Justice is being dragged in the way where those who devour bribes and give sentence with crooked judgements, take her. And she, wrapped in mist, follows to the city and haunts of the people, weeping, and bringing mischief to men, even to such as have driven her forth in that they did not deal straightly with her.

(ll. 225-237) But they who give straight judgements to strangers and to the men of the land, and go not aside from what is just, their city flourishes, and the people prosper in it: Peace, the nurse of children, is abroad in their land, and all-seeing Zeus never decrees cruel war against them. Neither famine nor disaster ever haunt men who do true justice; but light-heartedly they tend the fields which are all their care. The earth bears them victual in plenty, and on the mountains the oak bears acorns upon the top and bees in the midst. Their woolly sheep are laden with fleeces; their women bear children like their parents. They flourish continually with good things, and do not travel on ships, for the grain-giving earth bears them fruit.

(ll. 238-247) But for those who practise violence and cruel deeds far-seeing Zeus, the son of Cronos, ordains a punishment. Often even a whole city suffers for a bad man who sins and devises presumptuous deeds, and the son of Cronos lays great trouble upon the people, famine and plague together, so that the men perish away, and their women do not bear children, and their houses become few, through the contriving of Olympian Zeus. And again, at another time, the son of Cronos either destroys their wide army, or their walls, or else makes an end of their ships on the sea.

(ll. 248-264) You princes, mark well this punishment you also; for the deathless gods are near among men and mark all those who oppress their fellows with crooked judgements, and reck not the anger of the gods. For upon the bounteous earth Zeus has thrice ten thousand spirits, watchers of mortal men, and these keep watch on judgements and deeds of wrong as they roam, clothed in mist, all over the earth. And there is virgin Justice, the daughter of Zeus, who is honoured and reverenced among the gods who dwell on Olympus, and whenever anyone hurts her with lying slander, she sits beside her father, Zeus the son of Cronos, and tells him of men's wicked heart, until the people pay for the mad folly of their princes who, evilly minded, pervert judgement and give sentence crookedly. Keep watch against this, you princes, and make straight your judgements, you who devour bribes; put crooked judgements altogether from your thoughts.

(ll. 265-266) He does mischief to himself who does mischief to another, and evil planned harms the plotter most.

(ll. 267-273) The eye of Zeus, seeing all and understanding all, beholds these things too, if so he will, and fails not to mark what sort of justice is this that the city keeps within it. Now, therefore, may neither I myself be righteous among men, nor my son – for then it is a bad thing to be righteous – if indeed the unrighteous shall have the greater right. But I think that all-wise Zeus will not yet bring that to pass.

(ll. 274-285) But you, Perses, lay up these things within you heart and listen now to right, ceasing altogether to think of violence. For the son of Cronos has ordained this law for men, that fishes and beasts and winged fowls should devour one another, for right is not in them; but to mankind he gave right which proves far the best. For whoever knows the right and is ready to speak it, far-seeing Zeus gives him prosperity; but whoever deliberately lies in his witness and forswears himself, and so hurts Justice and sins beyond repair, that man's generation is left obscure thereafter. But the generation of the man who swears truly is better thenceforward.

(ll. 286-292) To you, foolish Perses, I will speak good sense. Badness can be got easily and in shoals: the road to her is smooth, and she lives very near us. But between us and Goodness the gods have placed the sweat of our brows: long and steep is the path that leads to her, and it is rough at the first; but when a man has reached the top, then is she easy to reach, though before that she was hard.

(ll. 293-319) That man is altogether best who considers all things himself and marks what will be better afterwards and at the end; and he, again, is good who listens to a good adviser; but whoever neither thinks for himself nor keeps in mind what another tells him, he is an unprofitable man. But do you at any rate, always remembering my charge, work, high-born Perses, that Hunger may hate you, and venerable Demeter richly crowned may love you and fill your barn with food; for Hunger is altogether a meet comrade for the sluggard. Both gods and men are angry with a man who lives idle, for in nature he is like the stingless drones who waste the labour of the bees, eating without working; but let it be your care to order your work properly, that in the right season your barns may be full of victual. Through work men grow rich in flocks and substance, and working they are much better loved by the immortals[8]. Work is no disgrace: it is idleness which is a disgrace. But if you work, the idle will soon envy you as you grow rich, for fame and renown attend on wealth. And whatever be your lot, work is best for you, if you turn your misguided mind away from other men's property to your work and attend to your livelihood as I bid you. An evil shame is the needy man's companion, shame which both greatly harms and prospers men: shame is with poverty, but confidence with wealth.

(ll. 320-341) Wealth should not be seized: god-given wealth is much better; for if a man take great wealth violently and perforce, or if he steal it through his tongue, as often happens when gain deceives men's sense and dishonour tramples down honour, the gods soon blot him out and make that man's house low, and wealth attends him only for a little time. Alike with him who does wrong to a suppliant or a guest, or who goes up to his brother's bed and commits unnatural sin in lying with his wife, or who infatuately offends against fatherless children, or who abuses his old father at the cheerless threshold of old age and attacks him with harsh words, truly Zeus himself is angry, and at the last lays on him a heavy requittal for his evil doing. But do you turn your foolish heart altogether away from these things, and, as far as you are able, sacrifice to the deathless gods purely and cleanly, and burn rich meats also, and at other times propitiate them with libations and incense, both when you go to bed and when the holy light has come back, that they may be gracious to you in heart and spirit, and so you may buy another's holding and not another yours.

(ll. 342-351) Call your friend to a feast; but leave your enemy alone; and especially call him who lives near you: for if any mischief happen in the place, neighbours come ungirt, but kinsmen stay to gird themselves[9]. A bad neighbour is as great a plague as a good one is a great blessing; he who enjoys a good neighbour has a precious possession. Not even an ox would die but for a bad neighbour. Take fair measure from your neighbour and pay him back fairly with the same measure, or better, if you can; so that if you are in need afterwards, you may find him sure.

(ll. 352-369) Do not get base gain: base gain is as bad as ruin. Be friends with the friendly, and visit him who visits you. Give to one who gives, but do not give to one who does not give. A man gives to the free-handed, but no one gives to the close-fisted. Give is a good girl, but Take is bad and she brings death. For the man who gives willingly, even though he gives a great thing, rejoices in his gift and is glad in heart; but whoever gives way to shamelessness and takes something himself, even though it be a small thing, it freezes his heart. He who adds to what he has, will keep off bright-eyed hunger; for it you add only a little to a little and do this often, soon that little will become great. What a man has by him at home does not trouble him: it is better to have your stuff at home, for whatever is abroad may mean loss. It is a good thing to draw on what you have; but it grieves your heart to need something and not to have it, and I bid you mark this. Take your fill when the cask is first opened and when it is nearly spent, but midways be sparing: it is poor saving when you come to the lees.

(ll. 370-372) Let the wage promised to a friend be fixed; even with your brother smile – and get a witness; for trust and mistrust, alike ruin men.

(ll. 373-375) Do not let a flaunting woman coax and cozen and deceive you: she is after your barn. The man who trusts womankind trust deceivers.

(ll. 376-380) There should be an only son, to feed his father's house, for so wealth will increase in the home; but if you leave a second son you should die old. Yet Zeus can easily give great wealth to a greater number. More hands mean more work and more increase.

(ll. 381-382) If your heart within you desires wealth, do these things and work with work upon work.

(ll. 383-404) When the Pleiades, daughters of Atlas, are rising[10], begin your harvest, and your ploughing when they are going to set [11]. Forty nights and days they are hidden and appear again as the year moves round, when first you sharpen your sickle. This is the law of the plains, and of those who live near the sea, and who inhabit rich country, the glens and dingles far from the tossing sea, – strip to sow and strip to plough and strip to reap, if you wish to get in all Demeter's fruits in due season, and that each kind may grow in its season. Else, afterwards, you may chance to be in want, and go begging to other men's houses, but without avail; as you have already come to me. But I will give you no more nor give you further measure. Foolish Perses! Work the work which the gods ordained for men, lest in bitter anguish of spirit you with your wife and children seek your livelihood amongst your neighbours, and they do not heed you. Two or three times, may be, you will succeed, but if you trouble them further, it will not avail you, and all your talk will be in vain, and your word-play unprofitable. Nay, I bid you find a way to pay your debts and avoid hunger.

(ll. 405-413) First of all, get a house, and a woman and an ox for the plough – a slave woman and not a wife, to follow the oxen as well – and make everything ready at home, so that you may not have to ask of another, and he refuses you, and so, because you are in lack, the season pass by and your work come to nothing. Do not put your work off till to-morrow and the day after; for a sluggish worker does not fill his barn, nor one who puts off his work: industry makes work go well, but a man who puts off work is always at hand-grips with ruin.

(ll. 414-447) When the piercing power and sultry heat of the sun abate, and almighty Zeus sends the autumn rains[12], and men's flesh comes to feel far easier, – for then the star Sirius passes over the heads of men, who are born to misery, only a little while by day and takes greater share of night, – then, when it showers its leaves to the ground and stops sprouting, the wood you cut with your axe is least liable to worm. Then remember to hew your timber: it is the season for that work. Cut a mortar[13] three feet wide and a pestle three cubits long, and an axle of seven feet, for it will do very well so; but if you make it eight feet long, you can cut a beetle[14] from it as well. Cut a felloe three spans across for a waggon of ten palms' width. Hew also many bent timbers, and bring home a plough-tree when you have found it, and look out on the mountain or in the field for one of holm-oak; for this is the strongest for oxen to plough with when one of Athena's handmen has fixed in the share-beam and fastened it to the pole with dowels. Get two ploughs ready and work on them at home, one all of a piece, and the other jointed. It is far better to do this, for if you should break one of them, you can put the oxen to the other. Poles of laurel or elm are most free from worms, and a share-beam of oak and a plough-tree of holm-oak. Get two oxen, bulls of nine years; for their strength is unspent and they are in the prime of their age: they are best for work. They will not fight in the furrow and break the plough and then leave the work undone. Let a brisk fellow of forty years follow them, with a loaf of four quarters[15] and eight slices[16] for his dinner, one who will attend to his work and drive a straight furrow and is past the age for gaping after his fellows, but will keep his mind on his work. No younger man will be better than he at scattering the seed and avoiding double-sowing; for a man less staid gets disturbed, hankering after his fellows.

(ll. 448-457) Mark, when you hear the voice of the crane[17] who cries year by year from the clouds above, for she give the signal for ploughing and shows the season of rainy winter; but she vexes the heart of the man who has no oxen. Then is the time to feed up your horned oxen in the byre; for it is easy to say: `Give me a yoke of oxen and a waggon,' and it is easy to refuse: `I have work for my oxen.' The man who is rich in fancy thinks his waggon as good as built already – the fool! He does not know that there are a hundred timbers to a waggon. Take care to lay these up beforehand at home.

(ll. 458-464) So soon as the time for ploughing is proclaimed to men, then make haste, you and your slaves alike, in wet and in dry, to plough in the season for ploughing, and bestir yourself early in the morning so that your fields may be full. Plough in the spring; but fallow broken up in the summer will not belie your hopes. Sow fallow land when the soil is still getting light: fallow land is a defender from harm and a soother of children.

(ll. 465-478) Pray to Zeus of the Earth and to pure Demeter to make Demeter's holy grain sound and heavy, when first you begin ploughing, when you hold in your hand the end of the plough-tail and bring down your stick on the backs of the oxen as they draw on the pole-bar by the yoke-straps. Let a slave follow a little behind with a mattock and make trouble for the birds by hiding the seed; for good management is the best for mortal men as bad management is the worst. In this way your corn-ears will bow to the ground with fullness if the Olympian himself gives a good result at the last, and you will sweep the cobwebs from your bins and you will be glad, I ween, as you take of your garnered substance. And so you will have plenty till you come to grey[18] springtime, and will not look wistfully to others, but another shall be in need of your help.

(ll. 479-492) But if you plough the good ground at the solstice[19], you will reap sitting, grasping a thin crop in your hand, binding the sheaves awry, dust-covered, not glad at all; so you will bring all home in a basket and not many will admire you. Yet the will of Zeus who holds the aegis is different at different times; and it is hard for mortal men to tell it; for if you should plough late, you may find this remedy – when the cuckoo first calls[20] in the leaves of the oak and makes men glad all over the boundless earth, if Zeus should send rain on the third day and not cease until it rises neither above an ox's hoof nor falls short of it, then the late-plougher will vie with the early. Keep all this well in mind, and fail not to mark grey spring as it comes and the season of rain.

(ll 493-501) Pass by the smithy and its crowded lounge in winter time when the cold keeps men from field work, – for then an industrious man can greatly prosper his house – lest bitter winter catch you helpless and poor and you chafe a swollen foot with a shrunk hand. The idle man who waits on empty hope, lacking a livelihood, lays to heart mischief-making; it is not an wholesome hope that accompanies a needy man who lolls at ease while he has no sure livelihood.

(ll. 502-503) While it is yet midsummer command your slaves: 'It will not always be summer, build barns.'

(ll. 504-535) Avoid the month Lenaeon[21], wretched days, all of them fit to skin an ox, and the frosts which are cruel when Boreas blows over the earth. He blows across horse-breeding Thrace upon the wide sea and stirs it up, while earth and the forest howl. On many a high-leafed oak and thick pine he falls and brings them to the bounteous earth in mountain glens: then all the immense wood roars and the beasts shudder and put their tails between their legs, even those whose hide is covered with fur; for with his bitter blast he blows even through them although they are shaggy-breasted. He goes even through an ox's hide; it does not stop him. Also he blows through the goat's fine hair. But through the fleeces of sheep, because their wool is abundant, the keen wind Boreas pierces not at all; but it makes the old man curved as a wheel. And it does not blow through the tender maiden who stays indoors with her dear mother, unlearned as yet in the works of golden Aphrodite, and who washes her soft body and anoints herself with oil and lies down in an inner room within the house, on a winter's day when the Boneless One[22] gnaws his foot in his fireless house and wretched home; for the sun shows him no pastures to make for, but goes to and fro over the land and city of dusky men[23], and shines more sluggishly upon the whole race of the Hellenes. Then the horned and unhorned denizens of the wood, with teeth chattering pitifully, flee through the copses and glades, and all, as they seek shelter, have this one care, to gain thick coverts or some hollow rock. Then, like the Three-legged One[24] whose back is broken and whose head looks down upon the ground, like him, I say, they wander to escape the white snow.

(ll. 536-563) Then put on, as I bid you, a soft coat and a tunic to the feet to shield your body, – and you should weave thick woof on thin warp. In this clothe yourself so that your hair may keep still and not bristle and stand upon end all over your body.

Lace on your feet close-fitting boots of the hide of a slaughtered ox, thickly lined with felt inside. And when the season of frost comes on, stitch together skins of firstling kids with ox-sinew, to put over your back and to keep off the rain. On your head above wear a shaped cap of felt to keep your ears from getting wet, for the dawn is chill when Boreas has once made his onslaught, and at dawn a fruitful mist is spread over the earth from starry heaven upon the fields of blessed men: it is drawn from the ever flowing rivers and is raised high above the earth by windstorm, and sometimes it turns to rain towards evening, and sometimes to wind when Thracian Boreas huddles the thick clouds. Finish your work and return home ahead of him, and do not let the dark cloud from heaven wrap round you and make your body clammy and soak your clothes. Avoid it; for this is the hardest month, wintry, hard for sheep and hard for men. In this season let your oxen have half their usual food, but let your man have more; for the helpful nights are long. Observe all this until the year is ended and you have nights and days of equal length, and Earth, the mother of all, bears again her various fruit.

(ll. 564-570) When Zeus has finished sixty wintry days after the solstice, then the star Arcturus[25] leaves the holy stream of Ocean and first rises brilliant at dusk. After him the shrilly wailing daughter of Pandion, the swallow, appears to men when spring is just beginning. Before she comes, prune the vines, for it is best so.

(ll. 571-581) But when the House-carrier[26] climbs up the plants from the earth to escape the Pleiades, then it is no longer the season for digging vineyards, but to whet your sickles and rouse up your slaves. Avoid shady seats and sleeping until dawn in the harvest season, when the sun scorches the body. Then be busy, and bring home your fruits, getting up early to make your livelihood sure. For dawn takes away a third part of your work, dawn advances a man on his journey and advances him in his work, – dawn which appears and sets many men on their road, and puts yokes on many oxen.

(ll. 582-596) But when the artichoke flowers[27], and the chirping grass-hopper sits in a tree and pours down his shrill song continually from under his wings in the season of wearisome heat, then goats are plumpest and wine sweetest; women are most wanton, but men are feeblest, because Sirius parches head and knees and the skin is dry through heat. But at that time let me have a shady rock and wine of Biblis, a clot of curds and milk of drained goats with the flesh of an heifer fed in the woods, that has never calved, and of firstling kids; then also let me drink bright wine, sitting in the shade, when my heart is satisfied with food, and so, turning my head to face the fresh Zephyr, from the everflowing spring which pours down unfouled thrice pour an offering of water, but make a fourth libation of wine.

(ll. 597-608) Set your slaves to winnow Demeter's holy grain, when strong Orion[28] first appears, on a smooth threshing-floor in an airy place. Then measure it and store it in jars. And so soon as you have safely stored all your stuff indoors, I bid you put your bondman out of doors and look out for a servant-girl with no children; – for a servant with a child to nurse is troublesome. And look after the dog with jagged teeth; do not grudge him his food, or some time the Day-sleeper[29] may take your stuff. Bring in fodder and litter so as to have enough for your oxen and mules. After that, let your men rest their poor knees and unyoke your pair of oxen.

(ll. 609-617) But when Orion and Sirius are come into mid-heaven, and rosy-fingered Dawn sees Arcturus[30], then cut off all the grape-clusters, Perses, and bring them home. Show them to the sun ten days and ten nights: then cover them over for five, and on the sixth day draw off into vessels the gifts of joyful Dionysus. But when the Pleiades and Hyades and strong Orion begin to set[31], then remember to plough in season: and so the completed year[32] will fitly pass beneath the earth.

(ll. 618-640) But if desire for uncomfortable sea-faring seize you; when the Pleiades plunge into the misty sea[33] to escape Orion's rude strength, then truly gales of all kinds rage. Then keep ships no longer on the sparkling sea, but bethink you to till the land as I bid you. Haul up your ship upon the land and pack it closely with stones all round to keep off the power of the winds which blow damply, and draw out the bilge-plug so that the rain of heaven may not rot it. Put away all the tackle and fittings in your house, and stow the wings of the sea-going ship neatly, and hang up the well-shaped rudder over the smoke. You yourself wait until the season for sailing is come, and then haul your swift ship down to the sea and stow a convenient cargo in it, so that you may bring home profit, even as your father and mine, foolish Perses, used to sail on shipboard because he lacked sufficient livelihood. And one day he came to this very place crossing over a great stretch of sea; he left Aeolian Cyme and fled, not from riches and substance, but from wretched poverty which Zeus lays upon men, and he settled near Helicon in a miserable hamlet, Ascra, which is bad in winter, sultry in summer, and good at no time.

(ll. 641-645) But you, Perses, remember all works in their season but sailing especially. Admire a small ship, but put your freight in a large one; for the greater the lading, the greater will be your piled gain, if only the winds will keep back their harmful gales.

(ll. 646-662) If ever you turn your misguided heart to trading and wish to escape from debt and joyless hunger, I will show you the measures of the loud-roaring sea, though I have no skill in sea-faring nor in ships; for never yet have I sailed by ship over the wide sea, but only to Euboea from Aulis where the Achaeans once stayed through much storm when they had gathered a great host from divine Hellas for Troy, the land of fair women. Then I crossed over to Chalcis, to the games of wise Amphidamas where the sons of the great-hearted hero proclaimed and appointed prizes. And there I boast that I gained the victory with a song and carried off an handled tripod which I dedicated to the Muses of Helicon, in the place where they first set me in the way of clear song. Such is all my experience of many-pegged ships; nevertheless I will tell you the will of Zeus who holds the aegis; for the Muses have taught me to sing in marvellous song.

(ll. 663-677) Fifty days after the solstice[34], when the season of wearisome heat is come to an end, is the right time for me to go sailing. Then you will not wreck your ship, nor will the sea destroy the sailors, unless Poseidon the Earth-Shaker be set upon it, or Zeus, the king of the deathless gods, wish to slay them; for the issues of good and evil alike are with them. At that time the winds are steady, and the sea is harmless. Then trust in the winds without care, and haul your swift ship down to the sea and put all the freight on board; but make all haste you can to return home again and do not wait till the time of the new wine and autumn rain and oncoming storms with the fierce gales of Notus who accompanies the heavy autumn rain of Zeus and stirs up the sea and makes the deep dangerous.

(ll. 678-694) Another time for men to go sailing is in spring when a man first sees leaves on the topmost shoot of a fig-tree as large as the foot-print that a cow makes; then the sea is passable, and this is the spring sailing time. For my part I do not praise it, for my heart does not like it. Such a sailing is snatched, and you will hardly avoid mischief. Yet in their ignorance men do even this, for wealth means life to poor mortals; but it is fearful to die among the waves. But I bid you consider all these things in your heart as I say. Do not put all your goods in hollow ships; leave the greater part behind, and put the lesser part on board; for it is a bad business to meet with disaster among the waves of the sea, as it is bad if you put too great a load on your waggon and break the axle, and your goods are spoiled. Observe due measure: and proportion is best in all things.

(ll. 695-705) Bring home a wife to your house when you are of the right age, while you are not far short of thirty years nor much above; this is the right age for marriage. Let your wife have been grown up four years, and marry her in the fifth. Marry a maiden, so that you can teach her careful ways, and especially marry one who lives near you, but look well about you and see that your marriage will not be a joke to your neighbours. For a man wins nothing better than a good wife, and, again, nothing worse than a bad one, a greedy soul who roasts her man without fire, strong though he may be, and brings him to a raw[35] old age.

(ll. 706-714) Be careful to avoid the anger of the deathless gods. Do not make a friend equal to a brother; but if you do, do not wrong him first, and do not lie to please the tongue. But if he wrongs you first, offending either in word or in deed, remember to repay him double; but if he ask you to be his friend again and be ready to give you satisfaction, welcome him. He is a worthless man who makes now one and now another his friend; but as for you, do not let your face put your heart to shame[36].

(ll. 715-716) Do not get a name either as lavish or as churlish; as a friend of rogues or as a slanderer of good men.

(ll. 717-721) Never dare to taunt a man with deadly poverty which eats out the heart; it is sent by the deathless gods. The best treasure a man can have is a sparing tongue, and the greatest pleasure, one that moves orderly; for if you speak evil, you yourself will soon be worse spoken of.

(ll. 722-723) Do not be boorish at a common feast where there are many guests; the pleasure is greatest and the expense is least[37].

(ll. 724-726) Never pour a libation of sparkling wine to Zeus after dawn with unwashen hands, nor to others of the deathless gods; else they do not hear your prayers but spit them back.

(ll. 727-732) Do not stand upright facing the sun when you make water, but remember to do this when he has set towards his rising. And do not make water as you go, whether on the road or off the road, and do not uncover yourself: the nights belong to the blessed gods. A scrupulous man who has a wise heart sits down or goes to the wall of an enclosed court.

(ll. 733-736) Do not expose yourself befouled by the fireside in your house, but avoid this. Do not beget children when you are come back from ill-omened burial, but after a festival of the gods.

(ll. 737-741) Never cross the sweet-flowing water of ever-rolling rivers afoot until you have prayed, gazing into the soft flood, and washed your hands in the clear, lovely water. Whoever crosses a river with hands unwashed of wickedness, the gods are angry with him and bring trouble upon him afterwards.

(ll. 742-743) At a cheerful festival of the gods do not cut the withered from the quick upon that which has five branches[38] with bright steel.

(ll. 744-745) Never put the ladle upon the mixing-bowl at a wine party, for malignant ill-luck is attached to that.

(ll. 746-747) When you are building a house, do not leave it rough-hewn, or a cawing crow may settle on it and croak.

(ll. 748-749) Take nothing to eat or to wash with from uncharmed pots, for in them there is mischief.

(ll. 750-759) Do not let a boy of twelve years sit on things which may not be moved[39], for that is bad, and makes a man unmanly; nor yet a child of twelve months, for that has the same effect. A man should not clean his body with water in which a woman has washed, for there is bitter mischief in that also for a time. When you come upon a burning sacrifice, do not make a mock of mysteries, for Heaven is angry at this also. Never make water in the mouths of rivers which flow to the sea, nor yet in springs; but be careful to avoid this. And do not ease yourself in them: it is not well to do this.

(ll. 760-763) So do: and avoid the talk of men. For Talk is mischievous, light, and easily raised, but hard to bear and difficult to be rid of. Talk never wholly dies away when many people voice her: even Talk is in some ways divine.

(ll. 765-767) Mark the days which come from Zeus, duly telling your slaves of them, and that the thirtieth day of the month is best for one to look over the work and to deal out supplies.

(ll. 769-768)[40] For these are days which come from Zeus the all-wise, when men discern aright.

(ll. 770-779) To begin with, the first, the fourth, and the seventh – on which Leto bare Apollo with the blade of gold – each is a holy day. The eighth and the ninth, two days at least of the waxing month[41], are specially good for the works of man. Also the eleventh and twelfth are both excellent, alike for shearing sheep and for reaping the kindly fruits; but the twelfth is much better than the eleventh, for on it the airy-swinging spider spins its web in full day, and then the Wise One[42], gathers her pile. On that day woman should set up her loom and get forward with her work.

(ll. 780-781) Avoid the thirteenth of the waxing month for beginning to sow: yet it is the best day for setting plants.

(ll. 782-789) The sixth of the mid-month is very unfavourable for plants, but is good for the birth of males, though unfavourable for a girl either to be born at all or to be married. Nor is the first sixth a fit day for a girl to be born, but a kindly for gelding kids and sheep and for fencing in a sheep-cote. It is favourable for the birth of a boy, but such will be fond of sharp speech, lies, and cunning words, and stealthy converse.

(ll. 790-791) On the eighth of the month geld the boar and loud-bellowing bull, but hard-working mules on the twelfth.

(ll. 792-799) On the great twentieth, in full day, a wise man should be born. Such an one is very sound-witted. The tenth is favourable for a male to be born; but, for a girl, the fourth day of the mid-month. On that day tame sheep and shambling, horned oxen, and the sharp-fanged dog and hardy mules to the touch of the hand. But take care to avoid troubles which eat out the heart on the fourth of the beginning and ending of the month; it is a day very fraught with fate.

(ll. 800-801) On the fourth of the month bring home your bride, but choose the omens which are best for this business.

(ll. 802-804) Avoid fifth days: they are unkindly and terrible. On a fifth day, they say, the Erinyes assisted at the birth of Horcus (Oath) whom Eris (Strife) bare to trouble the forsworn.

(ll. 805-809) Look about you very carefully and throw out Demeter's holy grain upon the well-rolled[43] threshing floor on the seventh of the mid-month. Let the woodman cut beams for house building and plenty of ships' timbers, such as are suitable for ships. On the fourth day begin to build narrow ships.

(ll. 810-813) The ninth of the mid-month improves towards evening; but the first ninth of all is quite harmless for men. It is a good day on which to beget or to be born both for a male and a female: it is never an wholly evil day.

(ll. 814-818) Again, few know that the twenty-seventh of the month is best for opening a wine-jar, and putting yokes on the necks of oxen and mules and swift-footed horses, and for hauling a swift ship of many thwarts down to the sparkling sea; few call it by its right name.

(ll. 819-821) On the fourth day open a jar. The fourth of the mid-month is a day holy above all. And again, few men know that the fourth day after the twentieth is best while it is morning: towards evening it is less good.

(ll. 822-828) These days are a great blessing to men on earth; but the rest are changeable, luckless, and bring nothing. Everyone praises a different day but few know their nature. Sometimes a day is a stepmother, sometimes a mother. That man is happy and lucky in them who knows all these things and does his work without offending the deathless gods, who discerns the omens of birds and avoids transgressions.

ENDNOTES:

(1) That is, the poor man's fare, like `bread and cheese'.

(2) The All-endowed.

(3) The jar or casket contained the gifts of the gods mentioned in l.82.

(4) Eustathius refers to Hesiod as stating that men sprung 'from oaks and stones and ashtrees'. Proclus believed that the Nymphs called Meliae ("Theogony", 187) are intended. Goettling would render: 'A race terrible because of their (ashen) spears.'

(5) Preserved only by Proclus, from whom some inferior MSS. have copied the verse. The four following lines occur only in Geneva Papyri No. 94. For the restoration of ll. 169b-c see "Class. Quart." vii. 219-220. (i.e., the version quoted by Proclus stops at this point, and restarts at l.170.).

(6) i.e. the race will so degenerate that at the last even a new-born child will show the marks of old age.

(7) Aidos, as a quality, is that feeling of reverence or shame which restrains men from wrong: Nemesis is the feeling of righteous indignation aroused especially by the sight of the wicked in undeserved prosperity (cf. "Psalms", lxxii. 1-19).

(8) The alternative version is: 'and, working, you will be much better loved both by gods and men; for they greatly dislike the idle.'

(9) i.e. neighbours come at once and without making preparations, but kinsmen by marriage (who live at a distance) have to prepare, and so are long in coming.

(10) Early in May.

(11) In November.

(12) In October.

(13) For pounding corn.

(14) A mallet for breaking clods after ploughing.

(15) The loaf is a flattish cake with two intersecting lines scored on its upper surface which divide it into four equal parts.

(16) The meaning is obscure. A scholiast renders 'giving eight mouthfulls'; but the elder Philostratus uses the word in contrast to 'leavened'.

(17) About the middle of November.

(18) Spring is so described because the buds have not yet cast their iron-grey husks.

(19) In December.

(20) In March.

(21) The latter part of January and earlier part of February.

(22) i.e. the octopus or cuttle.

(23) i.e. the darker-skinned people of Africa, the Egyptians or Aethiopians.

(24) i.e. an old man walking with a staff (the `third leg' – as in the riddle of the Sphinx).

(25) February to March.

(26) i.e. the snail. The season is the middle of May.

(27) In June.

(28) July.

(29) i.e. a robber.

(30) September.

(31) The end of October.

(32) That is, the succession of stars which make up the full year.

(33) The end of October or beginning of November.

(34) July-August.

(35) i.e. untimely, premature. Juvenal similarly speaks of 'cruda senectus' (caused by gluttony).

(36) The thought is parallel to that of 'O, what a goodly outside falsehood hath.'

(37) The 'common feast' is one to which all present subscribe. Theognis (line 495) says that one of the chief pleasures of a banquet is the general conversation. Hence the present passage means that such a feast naturally costs little, while the many present will make pleasurable conversation.

(38) i.e. 'do not cut your finger-nails'.

(39) i.e. things which it would be sacrilege to disturb, such as tombs.

(40) H.G. Evelyn-White prefers to switch ll. 768 and 769, reading l. 769 first then l. 768. – DBK

(41) The month is divided into three periods, the waxing, the mid-month, and the waning, which answer to the phases of the moon.

(42) i.e. the ant.

(43) Such seems to be the meaning here, though the epithet is otherwise rendered 'well-rounded'. Corn was threshed by means of a sleigh with two runners having three or four rollers between them, like the modern Egyptian "nurag".

AZILOTH BOOKS

Aziloth Books publishes a wide range of titles ranging from hard-to-find esoteric books - *Parchment Books* - to classic works on fiction, politics and philosophy - *Cathedral Classics*. Our newest venture is *Aziloth Books Children's Classics*, with vibrant new covers and illustrations to complement some of the world's very best children's tales. All our imprints are offered to the reader at a competitive price and through as many mediums and outlets as possible.

We are committed to excellent book production and strive, whenever possible, to add value to our titles with original images, maps and author introductions. With the premium on space in most modern dwellings, we also endeavour - within the limits of good book design - to make our products as slender as possible, allowing more books to be fitted into a given bookshelf area.

We are a small, approachable company and would love to hear any of your comments and suggestions on our plans, products, or indeed on absolutely anything.

Aziloth Books, Rimey Law, Rookhope, Co. Durham, DL13 2BL, England.
t: 01388-517600 e: info@azilothbooks.com w: www.azilothbooks.com

PARCHMENT BOOKS enshrines the concept of the oneness of all true religious traditions - that "the light shines from many different lanterns". Our list below offers titles from both eastern and western spiritual traditions, including Christian, Judaic, Islamic, Daoist, Hindu and Buddhist mystical texts, as well as books on alchemy, hermeticism, paganism, etc. By bringing together such spiritual texts, we hope to make esoteric and occult knowledge more readily available to those ready to receive it. We do not publish grimoires or titles pertaining to the left hand path. Titles include:

The Prophet; The Madman: Parables & Poems	Khalil Gibran
Abandonment to Divine Providence	Jean-Pierre de Caussade
Corpus Hermeticum	G. R. S. Mead (trans.)
The Holy Rule of St Benedict	St. Benedict of Nursia
The Confession of St Patrick	St. Patrick
The Outline of Sanity	G. K. Chesterton
An Outline of Occult Science	Rudolf Steiner
The Dialogue Of St Catherine Of Siena	St. Catherine of Siena
Esoteric Christianity; Thought-Forms*	Annie Besant
The Teachings of Zoroaster	Shapurji A. Kapadia
The Spiritual Exercises of St. Ignatius	St. Ignatius of Loyola
Daemonologie	King James of England
A Dweller on Two Planets	Phylos the Thibetan
Bushido*	Nitobe Inazo
The Interior Castle	St. Teresa of Avila
Songs of Innocence & Experience*	William Blake
The Secret of the Rosary	St. Louis Marie de Montfort
From Ritual to Romance	Jessie L. Weston
The God of the Witches	Margaret Murray
Kundalini – an occult experience	George S. Arundale
The Kingdom of God is Within You	Leo Tolstoy
The Trial and Death of Socrates	Plato
A Textbook of Theosophy	Charles W. Leadbetter
Chuang Tzu: Daoist Teachings	Chuang Tzu
Practical Mysticism	Evelyn Underhill
Tao Te Ching (Lao Tzu's 'Book of the Way')	Tzu, Lao
The Most Holy Trinosophia	Le Comte de St.-Germain
Tertium Organum	P. D. Ouspensky
Totem and Taboo	Sigmund Freud
The Kebra Negast	E. A. Wallis Budge
Esoteric Buddhism	Alfred Percy Sinnett
Demian: the story of a youth	Hermann Hesse

* with colour illustrations

Obtainable at all good online and local bookstores.
View Aziloth Books' full list at: www.azilothbooks.com

CATHEDRAL CLASSICS hosts an array of classic literature, from erudite ancient tomes to avant-garde, twentieth-century masterpieces, all of which deserve a place in your home. All the world's great novelists are here, Jane Austen, Dickens, Conrad, Arthur Machen and Henry James, brushing shoulders with such disparate luminaries as Sun Tzu, Marcus Aurelius, Kipling, Friedrich Nietzsche, Machiavelli, and Omar Khayam. A small selection is detailed below:

Frankenstein	Mary Shelley
Herland; With Her in Ourland	Charlotte Perkins Gilman
The Time Machine; The Invisible Man	H. G. Wells
Three Men in a Boat	Jerome K Jerome
The Rubaiyat of Omar Khayyam	Omar Khayyam
A Study in Scarlet; The Sign of the Four	Arthur Conan Doyle
The Picture of Dorian Gray	Oscar Wilde
Flatland	Edwin A. Abbott
The Coming Race	Bulwer Lytton
The Adventures of Sherlock Holmes	Arthur Conan Doyle
The Great God Pan	Arthur Machen
Beyond Good and Evil	Friedrich Nietzsche
England, My England	D. H. Lawrence
The Castle of Otranto	Horace Walpole
Self-Reliance, & Other Essays (series1&2)	Ralph W. Emmerson
The Art of War	Sun Tzu
A Shepherd's Life	W. H. Hudson
The Double	Fyodor Dostoyevsky
To the Lighthouse; Mrs Dalloway	Virginia Woolf
The Sorrows of Young Werther	Johann W. Goethe
Leaves of Grass - 1855 edition	Walt Whitman
Analects	Confucius
Beowulf	Anonymous
The Subjection of Women	John Stuart Mill
The Rights of Man	Thomas Paine
Progress and Poverty	Henry George
Captain Blood	Rafael Sabatini
Captains Courageous	Rudyard Kipling
The Meditations of Marcus Aurelius	Marcus Aureliu
The Social Contract	Jean Jacques Rousseau
War is a Racket	Smedley D. Butler
The Dead	James Joyce
The Old Wives' Tale	Arnold Bennett

Obtainable at all good online and local bookstores.
View Aziloth Books' full list at: www.azilothbooks.com

AZILOTH BOOKS | **CHILDREN'S Classics**

Aziloth Books is passionate about bringing the very best in children's classics fiction to the next generation of book-lovers. We believe in the transforming power of children's books to encourage a life-long love of reading, and publish only the best authors and illustrators. With its original design and outstanding quality, our highly successful list has something to suit every age and interest. Titles include:

The Railway Children	Edith Nesbit
Anne of Green Gables	Lucy Maud Montgomery
What Katy Did	Susan Coolidge
Puck of Pook's Hill	Rudyard Kipling
The Jungle Books	Rudyard Kipling
Just So Stories	Rudyard Kipling
Alice Through the Looking Glass	Charles Dodgson
Alice's Adventures in Wonderland*	Charles Dodgson
Black Beauty	Anna Sewell
The War of the Worlds	H. G Wells
The Time Machine	H. G .Wells
The Sleeper Awakes	H. G. Wells
The Invisible Man	H. G. Wells
The Lost World	Sir Arthur Conan Doyle
Gulliver's Travels*	Jonathan Swift
Catriona (David Balfour)	Robert Louis Stevenson
The Water Babies	Charles Kingsley
The First Men in the Moon	Jules Verne
The Secret Garden	Frances Hodgson Burnett
A Little Princess	Frances Hodgson Burnett
Peter Pan*	J. M. Barrie
The Song of Hiawatha*	Henry W. Longfellow
Tales from Shakespeare	Charles and Mary Lamb
The Wonderful Wizard of Oz	L. Frank Baum
The Complete Grimm's Fairy Tales	Jacob & Wilhelm Grimm
The Wind in the Willows*	Kenneth Grahame

*with colour illustrations

Obtainable at all good online and local bookstores.
View Aziloth Books' full list at: www.azilothbooks.com

The Carton Chronicles

*The Truth Charles Dickens Feared to Tell,
& the curious tale of Flashman's true father*

Morose, cynical and given to drink, Sydney Carton is one of Charles Dickens' most famous characters; a cold, dispassionate man, yet capable, in the final moments of A Tale of Two Cities, of sacrificing himself beneath the guillotine for Lucie, the woman he both loved and lost.

It now appears, however, that Dickens was being somewhat economical with the *actualité*.

Newly recovered documents, written in Carton's own hand, tell a far different tale. Sydney Carton survived his execution, only to find himself at the mercy of the monstrous Robespierre, author of the Paris Terror. His love Lucie languishes in a French prison, her husband dead, and Carton can ensure her survival only by becoming Robespierre's personal spy.

Reluctant, terrified and often drunk, Carton blunders his way through the major events of the French Revolution, grudgingly partaking in some of the blackest deeds of the Terror and, by a mixture of cowardice, bravado and luck, lending a hand in the fall of most of its leading figures. Kidnapped by the British, he finds himself a double agent, trusted by neither side. Our hero chronicles the slow decay of revolutionary ideals and, in passing, casts light on the true parentage of that sadistic villain of *Tom Brown's Schooldays*, the beastly Flashman.

PRAISE FOR KEITH LAIDLER'S WRITING:

Mr. Laidler's book is masterful, imaginative, superbly written and had me laughing out loud, scratching my head in awe at his prowess and at times positively squirming. By the time I finished the book I knew I had been in the company of someone quite extraordinary ... at times Mr Laidler's work rated alongside the best of Flashman, and (deep breath) at times even bettered him, especially in his later works.

Simply put, it is a masterpiece and I urge Mr Laidler to stop everything he is doing and get a second volume out as soon as is humanly possibly. This one will run and run and deservedly so... (Laurence Dunsmore, Amazon Review, verified purchaser).

"It is a riveting story, and Laidler tells it well" (Telegraph Review)

www.ingramcontent.com/pod-product-compliance
Lightning Source LLC
Chambersburg PA
CBHW071325040426
42444CB00009B/2088